SONS OF THUNDER

Neil Bradford has ridden motorcycles for over thirty years. He has owned Hondas, Kawasakis, Aprilias, Triumphs and a Ducati but always returns to flat-twin BMWs and currently rides a R1200GS Adventure. He works in publishing.

SONS OF THUNDER

WRITING FROM THE FAST LANE: A MOTORCYCLING ANTHOLOGY

SELECTED AND INTRODUCED
BY NEIL BRADFORD

MAINSTREAM
PUBLISHING

Copyright © Neil Bradford, 2012
All rights reserved
The moral right of the author has been asserted

First published in Great Britain in 2012 by
MAINSTREAM PUBLISHING company
(EDINBURGH) LTD
7 Albany Street
Edinburgh EH1 3UG

ISBN 9781780575247

A catalogue record for this book is available from the British Library

Designed by Peter Ward

Typeset in Minion by Pali
Falkirk, Stirlingshire

Printed and bound in Gre
MPG Books Group Ltd, E

1 3 5 7 9 10 8 6 4 2

For my daughter Kate

In speed we hurl ourselves beyond the body,
Our bodies cannot scale the heavens except in a fume of petrol
Bones. Blood. Flesh.
All pressed inward together.

T.E. LAWRENCE

CONTENTS

INTRODUCTION

T.E. Lawrence sought sanctuary at Clouds Hill near Bovington in Dorset. This small estate worker's cottage nestled at the base of the hills insulated by 'a moving forest of rhododendron'. When Lawrence first arrived it was run-down and required substantial work to make it habitable. Clouds Hill resonates with the personality, intellect and soul of the man. The cottage became a retreat from his public persona, a home for his magnificent library and extensive music collection, and a space where he could meet friends in private and write in peace. He made various changes to the simple original structure, the most characteristic of which was a thatched outhouse, which became the garage for Lawrence's motorcycles. It's not hard to imagine the short walk across the gravel path from the cottage, the release of the padlock and clasp sealing the garage doors and the subsequent roar of the exhaust as the latest of a succession of Brough Superiors was wheeled out of its den and brought to life. Lawrence had a total of seven Superiors commencing in 1922 and concluding in 1935 with the SS100 upon which he died. There was an eighth machine on order, which was never collected. Each bike was named by Lawrence. All the bikes were referred to as 'Boanerges' or 'Sons of Thunder' in Aramaic, but the naming had a sub-category 'George' to distinguish them further: a respectful nod to the owner and manufacturer, George Brough, with whom Lawrence shared a great friendship.

Lawrence's relationship with his motorcycles was intense and the machine was the exhilarating means of escape from the constrictions of the army camp:

> When my mood gets too hot and I find myself wandering beyond control I pull out my motor-bike and hurl it top speed through these unfit roads for hour after hour.

This feeling of release and exhilaration is one shared by all who have reached for the crash helmet, swept up the keys and opened the front door. The environment, climate and character of the road are all absorbed by the rider who makes corresponding physical adjustments to deal with the demands of every journey, whatever the length. This sensation is unique to the motorcyclist.

Each of the extracts within this collection communicates the emotional bond between rider and machine. The feeling of 'oneness' with the motorcycle is core. The rider becomes physically part of the bike rather than simply sitting astride the machine. There is the adolescent joy of Roald Dahl, the technical authority of L. J. K. Setright, the inexplicable desire, trepidation and ultimate resignation of Thomas McGuane and the exquisite prose of Melissa Holbrook Pierson, recording the arcane rites of the pre-flight check, ignition and subsequent take-off.

The modern motorcycle is a sophisticated construction with little in the way of roughly hewn edges such as the kick-starter, an inducement to injury and post-traumatic stress disorder, so well described by Matthew Crawford elsewhere in his book:

> Before taking that final kick, it is traditional to light a cigarette and set it dangling at an angle that suggests nonchalance. While you're at it, send up a little prayer

for fuel atomization. You wouldn't be riding a motorcycle if you weren't an optimist.

With *Jupiter's Travels* Ted Simon revived the genre for the post-Vietnam war generation, echoing the exploits of Robert Edison Fulton Jr. Lois Pryce follows in the pioneering tyre tracks of Theresa Wallach. Dan Walsh's caustic and revolutionary columns echo something of the unique character that was Hunter S. Thompson.

I ride a BMW R1200GS Adventure, a bike built to circumnavigate the globe in the manner of Ewan McGregor and Charley Boorman. But how often do I satisfy the wanderlust? A couple of months back, I had left work a little earlier than usual and pulled up at some traffic lights. A car stopped beside me and I felt a tug on my arm. When I looked down, the driver handed me a card which was printed with the images of three motorcyclists with the same bike as mine. The pictures were accompanied by an appeal to 'ride it somewhere awesome'. It appeared that the driver was about to embark with some like-minded friends on an expedition to Tashkent. We chatted until conversation was curtailed by the green light and he pulled away, assuring me that his previous long-range journey had gifted him a further ten years of life and that he intended to add to the positive balance.

This collection is that of an enthusiast for the motorcycle. I was enthralled and inspired by each of the contributors' experiences and hope that the reader of this collection is tempted to explore further. Meanwhile I need to understand my bike more, *feel* it more, believe in its ability to release something within me, reduce the spiritual overdraft and make a journey *somewhere awesome . . .*

Neil Bradford, London, April 2012

MELISSA HOLBROOK PIERSON

Extract from

THE PERFECT VEHICLE

Melissa Holbrook Pierson was born in Akron, Ohio, in 1957. She lives in New York state and is devoted to motorcycles, particularly those of the Italian Moto Guzzi marque. Her writing is exquisitely precise, lyrical and passionate, and communicates the emotional bond between the rider and the motorcycle. *The Perfect Vehicle* was widely praised on publication and is without doubt some of the finest writing inspired by the motorcycle.

At precisely this moment someone, somewhere, is getting ready to ride. The motorcycle stands in the cool, dark garage, its air expectant with gas and grease. The rider approaches from outside; the door opens with a whir and a bang. The light goes on. A flame, everlasting, seems to rise on a piece of chrome.

As the rider advances, leather sleeves are zipped down tight on the forearms, and the helmet briefly obliterates everything as it is pulled on, the chin strap buckled. This muffled weight with its own faint but permanent scent triggers recollection of the hours and days spent within it. Soft leather gloves with studded palms, insurance against the reflex of a falling body to put its hands out in midair, go on last.

The key is slipped into the ignition at the top of the steering head. Then the rider swings a leg over the seat and sits but keeps the weight on the balls of the feet. With a push from the thighs the rider rocks the bike forward once, again, picking up momentum until it starts to fall forward and down from the centre-stand. At this moment the rider pulls a lever with the first finger of the right hand, and the brake pads close like a vice on the front wheel's iron rotor. At the almost instantaneous release of the brake, the bike rises slightly from the forks, which had telescoped under the heft. Now the 450 pounds of metal, fluid and plastic rests in tenuous balance between the rider's legs; if it started to lean too much to one side, the weight that had lain it low in a state of grace would suddenly assert itself in a manic bid to meet the concrete with a crash. Inherently unstable at a standstill, the bike is waiting for the human to help it become its true self. Out there running, it can seem as solid as stone.

The key turns; the idiot lights glow. The green is for neutral gear, the red for the battery, another red for oil pressure. The starter button on the right handlebar, pressed, begins a whirring below. A simultaneous twist of the right grip pulls the throttle cables and the engine bleats, then gulps, then roars. There is contained fire within inches of the rider's knees. As the plugs in the two cylinders, posed in a 90-degree V, take their inestimably quick turns in sparking a volatile cocktail of fuel and compressed oxygen, the expanding gases forcing back the pistons, the machine vibrates subtly from side to side.

A flip of the headlight switch on the handlebar throws the garage walls to either side into theatrical relief. (The rider knows to run through all the lights – turn signals, tail light, brake lights tripped by hand and foot – to make sure they work, but is sometimes guilty of neglecting this step.) The rider pulls in the left-hand lever, then presses down with the left foot. There's a solid *chunk* as first gear engages.

In the neat dance that accomplishes many operations on a motorcycle – one movement to countered by another fro, an equilibrium of give and take – the squeezed clutch lever is slowly let out while the other hand turns the throttle grip down. The bike moves out into a brighter world where the sun startles the rider's eyes for a moment and washes everything in a continual pour.

Out in the early-morning street there is little traffic, for which the rider sends up thanks: on a bike, cars are irksome, their slow-motion ways infuriating. Pulling out of the drive, the rider shifts into second, this time with the boot toe under the lever to push it up. The small jolt of increased speed from the rear wheel is experienced in the seat, just as in the elastic pause when a horse gathers strength in its haunches before springing into a canter from the trot.

To warm up the tyres, the rider shifts so slightly in the seat it is hardly noticeable except to the bike, which dips left. Then quickly right again, then left, then right, until the machine is drawing a sinuous S down the road. They could dance like this all day, partnered closely and each anticipating the next step so surely it is not at all clear who is who.

As they reach the exurban limits and turn onto a narrow road that ascends among trees and infrequent stone houses set back in the shadows, other riders are accelerating up highway ramps; riding gingerly in first gear between two lanes of traffic jammed on a city bridge; hitting the dirt front-wheel-first after being launched from the top of a hillock in a field; trying to pass a motorhome making its all-too-gradual way into a national park; feeling a charge move from stomach to chest as the bike straightens up from the deepest lean it's yet entered; following three friends also on bikes into the parking lot of a diner for coffee; slowing down, cursing, to the shoulder because the clutch cable broke.

Today, on the way to a particular, longed-for destination, while joy taken in the wheels' consuming revolutions conflates with the desire to arrive, the journey becomes one of combined anticipation of its end and pleasure in its duration. Riding is an occupation defined by duplicities.

Take the numbers; seven million who ride stacked against 225 million who don't. (To get an idea of the minority status this number confirms, consider the fact that some twenty million Americans call themselves dedicated birdwatchers.) Those who ride are both alone and held tight in the fold of the elect. They draw together for protective warmth and take strange relish in needing to do so at all. The glue between these relative few can be tenacious: a rider travelling through a small town, spotted by a rider who lives there, is – because of this simple fact – invited home and given food and advice. A rider stopped by the roadside, even for a cigarette, prompts another biker to stop and ask if help is needed. At the very least, barring the occasional internecine feud that can make motorcyclists embody a sort of nationalism on wheels, they wave as they pass one another. It's as if they all came from the same small burg where street greetings are as obligatory as wearing clothes.

The road, constantly turning, constantly offers up the possibility of something unexpected around the bend – gravel in a tumult across the road, a car drifting over the yellow line, a dog maddened by the din from the pipes. The rider processes data from the road and its environs with a certain detachment, translating them nearly as quickly into physical response: eat or be eaten. There is no room in the brain for idle thought (except on the highway, when idle thoughts appear and float and reconfigure in endless array), and a biker can go for miles and miles without waking up to any sudden realization, including the one that nothing at all has been thought for miles and miles. The faster you ride, the more closed the circuit becomes, deleting everything but this second and the next, which are hurriedly merging. Having no past to regret and no future to await, the rider feels free. Looked at from this tight world, the other one with its gore and stickiness seems well polished and contained at last.

This peculiar physiological effect, common to all high-concentration pursuits, may be why one finds among motorcyclists a large number of people who always feel as if there were a fire lit under them when they are sitting still. When they're out riding, the wind disperses the flame so they don't feel the terrible heat. The duration of the ride starts to be the only time they know happiness, so they go on longer and longer or for more and more rides, while their families become more and more unhappy. For a few, those who become racers, relief is to be had only at 160 mph down a straightaway. They simultaneously embrace and deny the risk, the worst outcome of which is confined to accidents, that which is outside the norm. But the norm stands for much less here than it does elsewhere, and the realm of the accident is much larger. Instead of admitting to insanity to want to live in such a place, they imagine their way out of it: Well, if I fall, I'll land on the tyres or hay bales or grass berm. Then I'll pick up the bike and if it's not too badly damaged I'll finish the race. That's what they're prepared to allow. Their once colourful leathers are scuffed grey and held together with duct tape.

Every rider of a motorcycle lives with a little of the same denial, which is after all healthy and spares us from living in a world made entirely of dread. It is also the price of admission to a day like this. If the rider wants, the throttle can be cracked open so suddenly the handlebars yank the arms, threatening to run away with that paltry creature on back now reduced to hanging on and enjoying the ride.

The roar left to ring under the trees as the machine passes is like the laser arc of red drawn by a taillight in a long-exposure photograph at night. It is the ghost remnant of how the bike cleaved the air, and what the rider felt as gravity battled flight against the rider's body. The curves play games with the rider, and the rider is lost in the concentration it takes to match wits with an impressive opponent. How fast to enter this turn? The fact that you can be sadly mistaken is what gives the right choice its sweet taste.

But the rider has never known a fear quite like the one when riding just ahead is the object of deep affection. Flying along in tandem, an invisible wire stretched between them to connect the distance through a moving world, the one looks to the other like an insect clinging to the frenzied body of its prey. The rider, behind, watches this transformed human and sees right through the leathers to the tender skin as it looked while sleep was upon it. In one flash the rider sees how laughably easy it would be for something to happen. It is that pernicious distance between them that does the trick: a few yards that is an unbridgeable gap. Perhaps it's all projection – that the rider, looking toward the other, at once feels how vulnerable the self truly is. But isn't that what love is anyway? In hoping for the other, you realize how much you hope for yourself?

When things conspire – the traffic is thick and wild, the sun is leaving moment for moment, rain slicks the surface of the road – the rider best understands what can otherwise remain hidden: that a motorcyclist is both the happy passenger on an amusement park ride and its earnest operator. The rider splits into two, navigating between vacation and dire responsibility.

As the road leaves home farther and farther behind, it makes its own friendly advances to keep the rider happy: See, this is where you stopped your bike once and ate an apple from the tank bag and took off your boots to feel the damp grass beneath your socks; this is the place your beloved bought you a handful of fireballs when you stopped for gas. And there is always the chance that the unexpected around the bend may turn out not to be a danger to avoid, but a sight or smell that appears suddenly like a cheque in the mail.

Now, with a hundred miles on the clock, the going has taken on a life of its own. The rider has nearly forgotten what it means to sit anywhere but on this seat; the eyes are swinging back and forth in unchanging rhythm like sonar. Brake; slow; lean; heat up. Brake; slow; lean; heat up. Again and again until it's a rocking chair, a hundred freestyle laps, a hand absently stroking the skin.

The road's painted line, a vanishing point in reverse, is eaten up under the wheels, like a video game where the landscape flashes past while the vehicle stays put. The wind is a steady reassurance on the chest. The rider now becomes susceptible to white-line fever, which feels not so much like a need to continue on forever but as if all options for anything else have been removed. It is simple: the power to go, the power to stop, are as reduced as a metaphor and made to fit in one small hand. The rider, naturally, fears this state. And, keen on the perversity that always hides deep in pleasure, the rider, who is me, wants nothing more.

T.E. LAWRENCE writing as AIRCRAFTMAN ROSS
THE ROAD

Thomas Edward Lawrence was born in 1888 at Tremadoc in Wales. He achieved a First in Modern History at Oxford University and followed his passion for archaeology by working in the Middle East at various sites including the Hittite city of Carchemish in Syria. In 1915 he was posted to Cairo with British Military Intelligence and became an expert on Arab Affairs and crucially helped to organise the Arab Revolt. Lawrence recorded his wartime exploits against the Turks in the Middle East in *Seven Pillars of Wisdom* (1926), one of the classic accounts of twentieth-century warfare. In 1922 Lawrence resigned and joined the R.A.F., writing of his experiences in *The Mint* under the assumed name of 352087 Aircraftman Ross.

Lawrence wrote often of his abiding passion for motorcycles, frequently in letters to George Brough, the owner of the company that manufactured his favourite machine, the Brough Superior.

T.E. Lawrence, 'Lawrence of Arabia', crashed his motorcycle on 13 May 1935 near Bovington in Dorset, apparently attempting to avoid colliding with two children out on bicycles. He suffered serious head injuries, failed to regain consciousness and died six days later aged forty-six. His passing was lamented by the entire nation. He is buried at Moreton church, not far from his home at Clouds Hill in Dorset.

The extravagance in which my surplus emotion expressed itself lay on the road. So long as roads were tarred blue and straight; not hedged; and empty and dry, so long I was rich.

Nightly I'd run up from the hangar, upon the last stroke of work, spurring my tired feet to be nimble. The very movement refreshed them, after the day-long restraint of service. In five minutes my bed would be down, ready for the night: in four more I was in breeches and puttees, pulling on my gauntlets as I walked over to my bike, which lived in a garage-hut, opposite. Its tyres never wanted air, its engine had a habit of starting at second kick: a good habit, for only by frantic plunges upon the starting pedal could my puny weight force the engine over the seven atmospheres of its compression.

Boanerges' first glad roar at being alive again nightly jarred the huts of Cadet College into life. 'There he goes, the noisy bugger,' someone would say enviously in every flight. It is part of an airman's profession to be knowing with engines: and a thoroughbred engine is our undying satisfaction. The camp wore the virtue of my Brough like a flower in its cap. Tonight Tug and Dusty came to the step of our hut to see me off. 'Running down to Smoke, perhaps?' jeered Dusty; hitting at my regular game of London and back for tea on fine Wednesday afternoons.

Boa is a top-gear machine, as sweet in that as most

single-cylinders in middle. I chug lordily past the guard-room and through the speed limit at no more than sixteen. Round the bend, past the farm, and the way straightens. Now for it. The engine's final development is fifty-two horse-power. A miracle that all this docile strength waits behind one tiny lever for the pleasure of my hand.

Another bend: and I have the honour of one of England's straightest and fastest roads. The burble of my exhaust unwound like a long cord behind me. Soon my speed snapped it, and I heard only the cry of the wind which my battering head split and fended aside. The cry rose with my speed to a shriek: while the air's coldness streamed like two jets of iced water into my dissolving eyes. I screwed them to slits, and focused my sight two hundred yards ahead of me on the empty mosaic of the tar's gravelled undulations.

Like arrows the tiny flies pricked my cheeks: and sometimes a heavier body, some house-fly or beetle, would crash into face or lips like a spent bullet. A glance at the speedometer: seventy-eight. Boanerges is warming up. I pull the throttle right open, on the top of the slope, and we swoop flying across the dip, and up-down up-down the switchback beyond: the weighty machine launching itself like a projectile with a whirr of wheels into the air at the take-off of each rise, to land lurchingly with such a snatch of the driving chain as jerks my spine like a rictus.

Once we so fled across the evening light, with the yellow sun on my left, when a huge shadow roared just overhead. A Bristol Fighter, from Whitewash Villas, our neighbour aerodrome, was banking sharply round. I checked speed an instant to wave: and the slip-stream of my impetus snapped my arm and elbow astern, like a raised flail. The pilot pointed down the road towards Lincoln. I sat hard in the saddle, folded back my ears and went away after him, like a dog after a hare. Quickly we drew abreast, as the impulse of his dive to my level exhausted itself.

The next mile of road was rough. I braced my feet into the rests, thrust with my arms, and clenched my knees on the tank till its rubber grips goggled under my thighs. Over the first pot-hole Boanerges screamed in surprise, its mud-guard bottoming with a yawp upon the tyre. Through the plunges of the next ten seconds I clung on, wedging my gloved hand in the throttle lever so that no bump should close it and spoil our speed. Then the bicycle wrenched sideways into three long ruts: it swayed dizzily, wagging its tail for thirty awful yards. Out came the clutch, the engine raced freely: Boa checked and straightened his head with a shake, as a Brough should.

The bad ground was passed and on the new road our flight became birdlike. My head was blown out with air so that my ears had failed and we seemed to whirl soundlessly between the sun-gilt stubble fields. I dared, on a rise, to slow imperceptibly and glance sideways into the sky. There the Bif was, two hundred yards and more back. Play with the fellow? Why not? I slowed to ninety: signalled with my hand for him to overtake. Slowed ten more: sat up. Over he rattled. His passenger, a helmeted and goggled grin, hung out of the cock-pit to pass me the 'Up yer' Raf randy greeting.

They were hoping I was a flash in the pan, giving them best. Open went my throttle again. Boa crept level, fifty feet below: held them: sailed ahead into the clean and lonely country. An approaching car pulled nearly into its ditch at the sight of our race. The Bif was zooming among the trees and telegraph poles, with my scurrying spot only eighty yards ahead. I gained though, gained steadily: was perhaps five miles an hour the faster. Down went my left hand to give the engine two extra dollops of oil, for fear that something was running hot: but an overhead Jap twin, super-tuned like this one, would carry on to the moon and back, unfaltering.

We drew near the settlement. A long mile before the first houses I closed down and coasted to the cross-roads by the hospital. Bif caught up, banked, climbed and turned for home, waving to me as long as he was in sight. Fourteen miles from camp, we are, here: and fifteen minutes since I left Tug and Dusty at the hut door.

I let in the clutch again, and eased Boanerges down the hill along the tram-lines through the dirty streets and up-hill to the aloof cathedral, where it stood in frigid perfection above the cowering close. No message of mercy in Lincoln. Our God is a jealous God: and man's very best offering will fall disdainfully short of worthiness, in the sight of Saint Hugh and his angels.

Remigius, earthy old Remigius, looks with more charity on me and Boanerges. I stabled the steel magnificence of strength and speed at his west door and went in: to find the organist practising something slow and rhythmical, like a multiplication table in notes on the organ. The fretted, unsatisfying and unsatisfied lace-work of choir screen and spandrels drank in the main sound. Its surplus spilled thoughtfully into my ears.

By then my belly had forgotten its lunch, my eyes smarted and streamed. Out again, to sluice my head under the White Hart's yard-pump. A cup of real chocolate and a muffin at the teashop: and Boa and I took the Newark road for the last hour of daylight. He ambles at forty-five and when roaring his utmost, surpasses the hundred. A skittish motor-bike with a touch of blood in it is better than all the riding animals on earth, because of its logical extension of our faculties, and the hint, the provocation, to excess conferred by its honeyed untiring smoothness. Because Boa loves me, he gives me five more miles of speed than a stranger would get from him.

At Nottingham I added sausages from my wholesaler to the bacon which I'd bought at Lincoln: bacon so nicely sliced that each rasher meant a penny. The solid pannier-bags behind the saddle took all this and at my next stop, a farm, took also a felt-hammocked box of fifteen eggs. Home by Sleaford, our squalid, purse-proud, local village. Its butcher had six penn'orth of dripping ready for me. For months have I been making my evening round a marketing, twice a week, riding a hundred miles for the joy of it and picking up the best food cheapest, over half the countryside.

LETTER TO CHARLOTTE SHAW
24.8.1926

This morning dawned on me in Durham . . . after a mile or two I said to Boanerges 'We are going to hurry' . . . and thereupon laid back my ears like a rabbit, and galloped down the road. Galloped to some purpose too: Cranwell (160 miles) in 2 hours 58 minutes. It seemed to me that sixty-five miles an hour was a fitting pace. So we kept down to that where the road was not fit for more: but often we were ninety for two or three miles on end, with old B. trumpeting ha ha like a war-horse.

The rest of the north of England did not seem to love us. The Great North Road: (what a dream, what a drunkenness of delight of a name!) is, as you know, very wide and smooth, and straight. So that you can biff along it safely, without any tactics in meeting or overtaking traffic. Traffic this morning was mainly Morris Oxfords, doing their thirty up or down. Boa and myself were pioneers of the new order, which will do seventy or more between point and point. Like all pioneers we incurred odium. The Morris Oxfords were calculating on other traffic doing their own staid forty feet a second. Boa was doing 120. While they were thinking about swinging off the crown of the road to let him pass, he had leaped past them, a rattle and roar and glitter of polished nickel, with a blue button on top. They waved their arms wildly, or their sticks, in protest. Boa was round the next corner, or over the next-hill-but-two while they were spluttering. Never has Boa gone better. I kept on patting him, and opening his throttle, knowing all the while that in a month or two he will be someone else's, and myself in a land without roads or speed. If I were rich he should have a warm dry garage, and no work in his old age. An almost human machine, he is, a real prolongation of my own faculties: and so handsome and efficient. Never have I had anything like him.

LETTER TO GEORGE BROUGH
27.9.1926

Completed 100,000 miles, since 1922, on five successive Brough Superiors, and I'm going abroad very soon, so that I think I must make an end, and thank you for the road-pleasure I have got out of them. In 1922 I found George I (your old Mark I) the best thing I'd ridden, but George II (the 1922 SS100) is incomparably better. In 1925 and 1926 (George IV & V) I have not had an involuntary stop, and so have not been able to test your spares service, on which I drew so heavily in 1922 and 1923. Your present machines are as fast and reliable as express trains, and the greatest fun in the world to drive: and I say this after twenty years' experience of cycles and cars.

They are very expensive to buy, but light in upkeep (50–60 mpg of petrol, 4,000 mpg oil, 5,000–6,000 miles per outer cover, in my case) and in the four years I have made only one insurance claim (for less than £5) which is a testimony to the safety of your controls and designs. The SS100 holds the road extraordinarily. It's my great game on a really pot-holed road to open up to 70 mph or so and feel the machine gallop: and though only a touring machine it will do 90 mph at full throttle.

I'm not a speed merchant, but ride fairly far in the day

(occasionally 700 miles, often 500) and at a fair average, for the machine's speed in the open lets one crawl through the towns, and still average 40–42 miles in the hour. The riding position and the slow powerful turn-over of the engine at speeds of 500 odd give one a very restful feeling.

There, it is no good telling you all you knew before I did: they are the jolliest things on wheels.

ROALD DAHL

'MOTORBIKES'

from

MY YEAR

Roald Dahl was born in Wales to Norwegian parents in 1916. He related his early life in *Boy* (1984) and *Going Solo* (1986), which include memories of schooldays, travel, a love of motorcycles as well as an impressive war career as an 'ace' fighter pilot.

His output as a writer was phenomenal, numbering well over 50 books including poetry, film and television scripts as well as novels for children and adults including *Charlie and the Chocolate Factory* (1964), *The BFG* (1982), *The Witches* (1983) and *Matilda* (1988). Many of his books were illustrated by Quentin Blake and remain classics of children's fiction. He was one of the bestselling authors in the world.

Roald Dahl died in 1990 aged 74.

had bought my motorbike soon after I was sixteen. It was a second-hand Ariel 500cc and it cost me twenty-two pounds. It was a wonderful big powerful machine and when I rode upon it, it gave me an amazing feeling of winged majesty and of independence that I had never known before. Wherever I wished to go, my mighty Ariel would take me. Up to then, I had either had to walk or bicycle or buy a ticket for a bus or a train and it was a slow business. But now all I had to do was sling one leg over the saddle, kick the starter and away I went. I got the same feeling a few years later when I flew single-seater fighter planes in the war. Anyway, my plan now was to enliven the last term at Repton by secretly taking my motorbike with me. So on the first day of that summer term I rode it the hundred and fifty miles from our house in Kent to the village of Wilmington, which is about three miles from Repton. There I left it with a friendly garage owner together with my waders and helmet and goggles and wind jacket. Then I walked the rest of the way to school with my little suitcase.

Sunday afternoons were the only times we had free throughout the school week and most boys went for long walks in the countryside. But I took no long Sunday afternoon walks during my last term. My walks took me only as far as the garage in Wilmington where my lovely motorbike was hidden. There I would put on my disguise – my waders and helmet and goggles and wind jacket – and go sailing in a state of absolute bliss through the highways and byways of Derbyshire. But the greatest thrill of all was to ride at least once every Sunday afternoon slap through the middle of Repton village, sailing past the pompous prefects and the masters in their gowns and mortarboards. I felt pretty safe with my big goggles covering half of my face, although I will admit that on one famous occasion I got a twist in my stomach when I found myself motoring within a couple of yards of the terrifying figure of the headmaster, Dr Geoffrey Fisher himself, as he strode with purposeful step towards the chapel. He glared at me as I rode past, but I don't think it would have entered his brainy head for one moment that I was a member of the school. Don't forget that those were the days when schools like mine were merciless places where serious misdemeanours were punished by savage beatings that drew blood from your backside. I am quite sure that if I had ever been caught, that same headmaster would have thrashed me within an inch of my life and would probably have expelled me into the bargain. That is what made it so exciting. I never told anyone, not even my best friend, where I went on my Sunday walks. I had learnt even at that tender age that there are no secrets unless you keep them to yourself, and this was the greatest secret I had ever had to keep in my life so far.

TED HUGHES

A MOTORBIKE

Ted Hughes was born in Yorkshire in 1930. A poet of extraordinary range and authority, he was appointed Poet Laureate in 1984 and received the Order of Merit in 1998 when his final collection, *Birthday Letters*, was published and which subsequently won the Whitbread Prize, the T.S. Eliot Prize and the Forward Prize.

He died of cancer in 1998 aged 68.

We had a motorbike all through the war
In an outhouse – thunder, flight, disruption
Cramped in rust, under washing, abashed, outclassed
By the Brens, Bombs, the Bazookas elsewhere.

The war ended, the explosions stopped.
The men surrendered their weapons
And hung around limply.
Peace took them all prisoner.
They were herded into their home towns.
A horrible privation began
Of working a life up out of the avenues
And the holiday resorts and the dance-halls.

Then the morning bus was as bad as any labour truck,
The foreman, the boss, as bad as the S.S.
And the ends of the street and the bends of the road
And the shallowness of the shops and the shallowness of the beer
And the sameness of the next town
Were as bad as electrified barbed wire.
The shrunk-back war ached in their testicles
And England dwindled to the size of a dog-track.

So there came this quiet young man
And he bought our motorbike for twenty pounds.
And he got it going, with difficulty.
He kicked it into life – it erupted

Out of the six year sleep, and he was delighted.
A week later, astride it, before dawn,
A misty frosty morning,
He escaped

Into a telegraph pole
On the long straight west of Swinton.

L.J.K. SETRIGHT

Extract from

LONG LANE WITH TURNINGS

L.J.K. Setright was born in London in 1931. Best known for his regular articles in *Car* magazine and subsequently the occasional column in *Bike* magazine and the *Independent*, he also wrote, edited and compiled over twenty books.

Erudite and eccentric, this unique personality loved cars and motorcycles and wrote sublime technical prose, provocative, analytical, marginally lunatic, yet always guaranteed to grab your attention. This extract is taken from his unfinished memoir, *Long Lane with Turnings*.

He died in September 2005.

It had been painfully clear to me that girls did not like the Cloverleaf. The fact that it offered them no protection from the weather was only one reason why, and reminds me that the maximum speed when protecting myself from heavy rain with an opened umbrella was impractically low at 18mph. It was also painfully clear to me that so long as I remained hard up I had no right to be consorting with girls anyway, and that a motorcycle seating only me would be a suitable deterrent to both sides. I had enjoyed riding my brother's vintage Triumph; I had enjoyed a friend's modern Ariel Red Hunter, a lively sporting 500 single with a sprung heel; but the motorcycle for which I had long and truly yearned was the Douglas Ninety Plus.

When it first appeared in 1949, it was the most modern motorcycle in the world – and this at a time when everywhere there were designers keen to whet their ambitions upon the stony face of tradition, to issue a futurist manifesto that would snatch the motorcycle out of its straits of habitual thinking and set it refreshed by novel forms and unfamiliar details upon a socially broadened and theoretically uninhibited new course. Unfortunately this movement, which had actually been evident by 1938 but had been stifled by the events of soon-succeeding years, was characterized more by stylistic effrontery than by engineering nicety; but the Douglas was outstanding in both respects, its appearance the natural and proper expression of the technical advances with which its specification bristled.

In vain might sniffy historians dismiss its fully-looped frame, trailing-arm rear suspension and horizontally opposed twin-cylinder engine as mere echoes of the ABC which, designed by Granville Bradshaw a generation and a half earlier, had inspired BMW copyists to start making motorcycles. The Douglas was streets ahead of that as of everything else. Its springing was of progressive rate at both ends, by torsion bars for the rear and by taper-ground helical coils inside the tremendously rigid front forks with their leading bottom links. This was a chassis undaunted by obstacles: works riders used to demonstrate it by riding four times on and off a four inch kerb at 30mph. Here was steering that needed no damper: customers might buy one for £3 extra, if only for the sake of appearances, but would soon learn never to let it interfere.

Here, moreover, was a machine which – by virtue of a low centre of mass, a comfortably long wheelbase and a structurally stiff chassis, all assuring excellent roadholding – could exploit really good brakes. Within the front wheel was a liberally finned and copiously ventilated drum brake of exceptional size: the total friction area of the brakes on the 90+ was, as I will ever remember, no less than 42 in^2, practically double what most bikes could offer, when even the big-twin Vincent – bigger, heavier and faster, and endowed with two brake-drums to each wheel – mustered only 36.

Exploiting such braking gave me many a chuckle. Having measured the bike's ability to stop at a rate of 1.2g (in 25ft from 30mph) and to do it repeatedly and reliably, I would come rushing up to T-junctions at such a speed that traffic on the main road would screech to a halt, convinced that this silly young man on his dangerous motorcycle could never stop in time and was about to have an accident. Thus offered a road clear of moving hazards, I could ride into the junction and away without hindrance. Alternatively, if the approaching driver was as silly as me and kept on coming, I could always stop in time.

That was when everything was in adjustment and working properly. When it was not, there was the most frightful judder which threatened to tear everything asunder, including the laws of probability. The Douglas was like that in most respects: life with it was a succession of brief episodes of utter bliss punctuating long and bewildering periods of fettling and frustration.

It was hardly to be wondered at. The design might have been good by the standards of its time (by which I mean particularly the use of stress-inducing lugs for joining the various tubes of the frame, for this was before the days of welded joints), but the thing was poorly made from shoddy materials – and that, too, was not surprising, for the 90+ was created at a time when the Douglas company was in receivership. The touring model, the Mark V upon which the 90+ was based, had been too modern in concept for the woefully ignorant and bitterly reactionary British motorcycling public of the day, and Douglas paid the price, ending a proud history (dating back to 1906) of good and much-loved motorcycles in the ignominy of making Vespa scooters under licence. Considering that the firm was in the hands of the receivers when the 90+ was born, it was a marvel that the poor thing should ever have seen the light of day.

Yet the makers contrived to give it an extensively reworked engine, happy up to 7500 rev/min and capable of at least 25bhp (which was a good 20 per cent more than the average road-going 350 in those days), with a flyweight clutch and a beautiful close-ratio gearbox behind it. The ability to reach 87mph in third gear, 77 in second and 55 in bottom gear far outweighed any question of what the Plus might be beyond the Ninety.

Ironically, the ride I most remember did not involve much of that sort of thing. One high summer day I was riding to Canterbury, where I had been engaged to play in a scratch orchestra (with some very good players in the wind sections) for a morning rehearsal and afternoon performance of Elgar's *The Dream of Gerontius* in the cathedral. With my clarinet strapped behind me I got almost to Rochester to encounter the tail of what proved to be a six-mile queue. As carefully as one does in such circumstances, I rode past it all – and was dismayed by the anger and hostility of all those stationary motorists, blaring their horns or even waving fists at me. There was no way in which I could have been harming them, but the thought that I was going and they were not aroused furious jealousy. Even on a good motorcycle, the world can be a sad place . . .

A lot of work was done on my Douglas, most of it necessary and all of it desirable, and I learned a few things in the process – most importantly, the need for good tyres. Of all the amendments I made, the most productive was to replace the original spidery steel wheels with 19-inch light-alloy racing rims and fit racing tyres, which I discovered made improvements to the steering and handling beyond all my expectations.

The tyres were the worst feature of my next motorcycle, bought to keep me mobile at a time when I had quite despaired of the Douglas – though not so finally as to discard it. Bought new in 1960 (I never did repay Mother's loan, and still wonder whether she expected it), it was an Ariel Arrow, and once again it was derived from an exemplary modern design to which the British motorcyclist at large responded with his usual obstinate refusal to entertain nonconformist design. The Ariel Leader had

a couple of years earlier been the most modern motorcycle ever
– in the sense that the Citroën DS of 1955 was the most modern
car ever. The most obvious of its attributes was the comprehensive
weather protection (screen, fairing, and deeply valanced
mudguards), intended to allow a rider to go out without being
dressed like a deep-sea diver; but the most important was the
pressed-steel chassis, formed as a monocoque backbone of
generous proportions and admirable stiffness. Ariel did better
business when they issued a 'naked' version, somewhat lighter
and £30 cheaper, which they called the Arrow: the engine was
the same simple 250cm^3 two-stroke twin, and the bike still
displayed the sprightliness and quick handling of the Leader.

It also displayed the miserable workmanship of the smug
British industry which produced it: ovality of the brake drums
and a general disposition to rust were the worst offences. Worse
still was an error of judgement: when they specified 16-inch
wheels and quite large-section tyres (at a time when skinny tyres
on 19-inch wheels were the norm), they evidently feared that
the typical British customer would blame them if the rate of
tyre wear proved high. Accordingly, Dunlop were instructed to
produce a tyre of hard-wearing specification, and the tread
compound was therefore (since such was the trade-off in those
days when the rubber industry still had plenty to learn) almost
incapable of coming to grips with wet road surfaces. The Arrow
would have me off and sliding down the road on my ear if
someone so much as spat on the road. Racing people who
adapted the Arrow for competition threw those nice little rims
away and substituted nasty big conventional ones, because proper
grippy tyres were available for them. I simply grew frightened
of riding in the wet, and after a couple of years decided to get
rid of the thing.

By that time I had taken a bigger and more momentous decision. I had realized, after a couple of years at it, that the practice of the law did not suit me. As an academic subject I had found the law fascinating, but I hated its practical application, sullied with commerce, personal animosities, and onerous procedures serving no purpose but the perpetuation of some accident of history. Finding it so uncongenial, I realized at last that since I did not like it I should never be a success at it. At the end of 1960 I gave it up – one of the very best things I ever did – and prepared to make a fresh start.

ROBERT EDISON FULTON JR.

Extract from

ONE MAN CARAVAN

Robert Edison Fulton Jr. was born in Manhattan, New York, in 1909 into a family of successful businessmen and innovators. His father was the president of the Mack Trucks company and his grandfather and uncle established and developed a transportation service that was to evolve into the Greyhound Bus Line.

Having graduated from Harvard with a degree in architecture, he spent a further year at the University of Vienna. Whilst at a dinner party in London, imbued with the pioneer spirit but perhaps trying to get the attention of an attractive female guest, he stated that he intended to go around the world on a motorcycle rather than sail home to the U.S. It so happened that the president of the Douglas motorcycle company was also a guest, overheard the remark and immediately offered Fulton the use of one of his company's machines. In 1932 he left London on a journey which was to cover 25,000 miles and take 18 months, and which he recorded on film as well as in the book *One Man Caravan*.

Robert Edison Fulton Jr. died in 2004 at the age of 94.

Evening again. The day, a long and hot one, was almost over. It had been another 'desert day.' Dull? Far from it, for the days were filled with variety . . . principally the variety of spills. Those spills were classics, each one a little work of art complete in its frame. The thick dust threw the motorcycle unpredictably. I might travel for an hour without a single mishap and then within the next sixty minutes have six spills. I had an average of fifteen a day during the twenty-six-day trek across Turkey.

This particular day had been one of the many little worries. The clutch had not behaved at all decently, jamming frequently as the dust penetrated the mechanism, making it practically impossible to stop . . . except by capsizing, and then a matter of running through the thick dirt with the heavy machine in gear to start it again. Needless to say I often found myself going in circles, back the way I came, in any direction just to *keep going*, while making up my mind. And there had been many small decisions to make in choosing the route among many forking, branching, crossing trails and tracks. In the dimming light I scanned the horizon. Little wonder no village appeared.

But something far stranger did. At first, in the distance and half-light, it was a shapeless mass, a low, long white thing, a humped thing . . . On approaching, it gradually took form: a bridge, a brand new concrete bridge in the middle of a desert of dust. There was no road onto it, surely none off it, and definitely no water under it. It spanned a *wadi* some 200 feet wide, a dried-up river-bed which in the rainy season would be a swift torrent. Its surface was broad and smooth and, as the wheels emerged from the dust, the whole machine seemed to surge forward with life. It was like the marvelous lull after the dentist has drilled and drilled. It was now almost dark. Ducking behind windshield and luggage rack, I could just reach the switch. The headlight flickered once and then flashed bright to disclose, directly beneath me – emptiness!

Automatically the brake jammed, the machine twisted. But already I was on the brink of blackness. A span was missing! All of which I realized as the front wheel spun into space, the engine roared as the rear wheel left the ground . . . and everything went out.

Several hours must have elapsed. The sound of the engine was still ringing in my ears and things were reeling. Through my head kept jerking the name: 'Providence, Providence, Providence.' This was followed by the image of a crowd of idle onlookers laughing at my plight. I tried to open my eyes but shut them quickly as the effort produced further reeling and more 'Providences . . .' Then the merry-go-round subsided and I began to lavish self-pity in huge doses. Out of the mental haze gradually came the realization that this was not like going into a ditch at Providence. This was desert; this was dusty Turkish desert. There was only one similarity . . . the motorcycle.

The sudden thought and remembrance of what had occurred brought me to a sitting position so quickly that a dozen Turks went reeling into a corner in a confused heap.

I was in a tiny mud-room full of jabbering humanity . . . and the motorcycle. As I later discovered they had carried both machine and rider (the former weighing over 750 pounds), more than half a mile from the river bed to their village. Fortunately, as I also later discovered, though the fall had been over fifteen feet, both of us had landed on a sandy spot and, except for scratches and bruises and a few dents acquired from scattered rocks, no real damage was done.

One arm felt stiff and there was a shallow cut on the left hand. The left side of my head felt sore, but otherwise I could discover no indication of anything broken. The population sat quietly through a crude first-aid performance, consisting mainly of the stinging procedure of pouring iodine over every raw spot. But they were too curious to remain long silent. A patriarchal figure, no doubt the head man of the village, leaned forward. His words I could not understand but their meaning was unmistakable. It was a question, I was a stranger and consequently it could mean only one thing: 'Who was I and from where had I come?' I reached for the map.

In the flickering lamplight they made an unforgettable sight, crowded into the little room, a rising wall of heads to the very roof corners. Here and there the smooth skin of youth shone in sharp contrast to a weather-beaten, grooved face of age. A dozen pairs of curious eyes, softened by glaring sun and flying dirt, peered from below ragged caps and unruly hair. Bare legs and feet hard as leather protruded from tattered cloth. They were poor all right – poor in money, poor in material, but far from poor in heart. There was a kindliness and understanding about them which never comes with fighting for money but which comes only in living with the elements, the sun, sky and earth, adapting one's philosophy to the elemental, unaccountable ways.

Motionless the group waited for my reply. 'Sakchegeuzu,'

I read from the map. For a moment there was no sound . . . perhaps they hadn't understood. I tried again. 'Sakchegeuzu!' They had understood the first time. They looked at each other in alarm.

'Oh! Oh! Oh!' The patriarch threw his arms in the air. 'Allah be praised you are still alive! Sakchegeuzu! A terrible place! Terrible people! Robbers, cut-throats, thieves' . . . a description even more graphic than its predecessor.

On and on he went as again my mind wandered and hummed with a row of 'Providences.' Too well I knew the content of his diatribe. Had he ever been to Sakchegeuzu? 'No.' Did he know any of its inhabitants? 'No!' He had only heard of them . . . so long ago he couldn't even remember? 'Yes.' It was the same story I had listened to so many times since leaving London, the same one to be heard so many times on the 'way 'round,' the world's most international story.

Next morning I awoke to the stern realization that this was certainly far different from the aftermath of the first of all my motorcycle spills. Out here I couldn't expect a brief parental scolding and then lots of pampering for my injuries. I would have to pull myself together and get going. This was only Turkey. I was going around the world. I would have to touch all the bases or the umpire would call me out.

Painful stiffness made movement somewhat of an agony. But gradually I got over to the motorcycle. There the only damage I could find was a slightly bent front fork which thereafter tended to turn the machine in circles to the right.

But on checking the engine I was confronted by a major catastrophe, an oil streak along the side of the cylinders. The crankcase was virtually empty. While the machine had lain on its side for several hours after the spill the hot oil had quickly leaked out through the 'breather.' Fortunately there was still plenty of gasoline but even my mere extra quart of oil had been consumed since leaving the last general-store/filling station. Now the nearest source of supply was over fifty miles ahead. I would either have to walk the hundred mile round-trip, half way with a gallon of oil on my head . . . or what? And then, too, it was already late September. The rainy season was due any day, the dirty Turkish rainy season. No imagination was needed to picture what becomes of that dust desert when even so much as a shower crosses it. If the annual rains once caught up with me, it would be journey's end. Something had to be done . . . immediately.

A dozen old men, as many children and mud huts, what on earth could *be done* with them? And only the sign language in common. But at least they had proved good listeners.

'Look, must have oil. One gallon oil, half gallon, any amount, must have!'

I stuck the finger in the oil-sump to exhibit some of the precious bit that remained. Not a sign of understanding.

I said *oil* in every imaginable fashion: 'oil,' 'oeul,' 'huile,' and a dozen others . . . still no understanding. In fact only utter boredom, the elders rose and went off mumbling, leaving only a lot of howling, impish boys.

But it had always been the youngsters who understood quickest when there were road-difficulties. Maybe they could think of something now? A special demonstration followed, each being allowed to stick his stubby fingers into the crankcase and scrape the last oily remnants from the walls. They looked at it, they smelt it, some even tasted it, but not one looked as though there was even a thought in his head.

There seemed no alternative . . . a hundred miles over that dry and arid desert, and the last half with a clumsy gallon can.

Watching a little fellow struggle with an enormous jug, his legs wobbling like straws, I had visions of that return trip. Suddenly, when only a few feet away, the load became too much for him. With a rush, jug and all, he landed in my lap.

'Yagh!' he cried.

'Oil!' I echoed. It was golden-yellow, it was thick, it was viscous . . . in fact it was oil, even though it smelled. 'Mustard oil!' The youngster beamed. Leave it to the kids, they could find a way out of anything.

The crankcase was quickly filled and the machine packed to go. As if by magic the whole village seemed to convene. But I was too busy worrying whether or not the oil would lubricate. A kick of the starter, a roar, and the engine was running, and continued for several minutes. I watched the pressure gauge. The needle rose. Everything was humming smoothly and didn't seem to be overheating. I turned exultantly to the crowd. Half of them were shedding enormous tears. It brought a lump to my throat to see those kindly people so sad to see me go. I would never forget them. Then suddenly the wind changed and I too burst forth. Clouds of smoke issued from the exhaust. I quickly stopped the motor. MUSTARD GAS!

But the experiment had been satisfactory. The oil had lubricated. If only I could keep ahead of the fumes for the next fifty miles . . . and if I couldn't . . . well there would have been no walking anyway!

THERESA WALLACH

Extract from

THE RUGGED ROAD

Theresa Wallach was born in London in 1903. Early on she became exposed to the world of motorcycling through friends in the industry and, unknown to her parents, learnt to ride to a high standard. Despite the sexual discrimination that was customary in 1930s England, Theresa's skills could not be denied and she entered and won numerous competitions.

In 1935, along with her friend, Florence Blenkiron, she embarked upon an extraordinary and gutsy motorcycle expedition when they rode from London to Cape Africa on a 600cc Panther motorcycle/sidecar combination and trailer, a feat recorded in her book *The Rugged Road*.

In 1939 she won the British Motorcycle Racing Club Gold Star for lapping the classic Brooklands race circuit on a 350cc Norton at over 100 mph. During the war she served as a mechanic and became the first female dispatch rider in the British Army.

Theresa Wallach died in 1998.

The staccato noise of our motorcycle, which by now had lost its silencer, aroused drowsy folk from their midday siesta as we rolled to a standstill in Tamanrhasset. Arabs and Tuaregs gathered around us to see the strangers riding a horse-on-wheels. This was the first motorcycle to reach here – they had never seen one before. Being tired and weary after six days' hard riding for 250 miles and the climb up here, only just within our breakdown contract limit, we wanted to report to the Captain of this region as soon as possible. A Frenchman inside the mud building came from behind a coloured bead-curtain and we asked him the usual question. 'Where is the Captain, please?' Speaking slowly in French, so we could understand most of what he said, he replied, 'the Captain will come soon'. Then, loud and clear, we heard the soul-stirring bugle-call 'taran-tara' played by a Legionnaire in the rarefied air, high in the Hoggar Massif. It announced the end of the mid-day siesta and the Captain returned to duty and daily life resumed.

A friendly Captain greeted us with hand-shakes. He was not offended by our not understanding much of his French, but he muttered something about 'a foolish expedition'. Kindly, he said we may stay in the traveller's rest shelter without charge.

The typical desert shelter, very clean inside, had mud walls, open gap windows and an earth floor, partitioned by archways into four cubicles each with two folding beds and two chairs. I sat down on one of the folding beds to rest, and true to form, it folded, plonk!, onto the ground. This time we had a good laugh about it, for it was hardly like other mishaps along the way which had not been so amusing.

The Captain of this mountainous region was of the firm, soldierly sort. Although our days here were on the go, the most tiresome was the mental part in persuading him to let us go the remaining five hundred miles to Agadez, the last oasis. This was his territory and although we had the permit, he would not let us go into the Dunes of Jadal. His objection was our trailer. However, he was reasonable and said he would allow us to proceed if our trailer was taken off. By this time we were wise in the ways of the authorities and officials, who from the very beginning had disapproved of our venture, and we left the Captain at his desk. We went to the desert vehicle garage which, we thought, would be the only place to solve our problem. At first the *directeur* of the garage spoke Arabic, then he spoke French and our discussion continued with words spoken slowly, like an elementary class. 'I look at it!', he said coming outside to see the motorcycle and sidecar with its trailer standing near a bus, into which merchandise, bags and baggage were being loaded for its run to Agadez. 'Non', he said, 'we cannot tow it,' we understood him to say, 'it will fall to pieces!', meaning that it was not strong enough to be pulled behind the bus at speed over rough ground for a long distance. Blenk and I were inclined to agree that we might lose the trailer and everything in it so we tried hard to convey the urgency of our request. The trailer was not very wide, so we asked 'could it be lifted to lay the wheels up on the roof of the bus and lashed securely with our rope?' 'Yes!' for this idea, he agreed. We were allowed to ride the motorcycle and sidecar without the trailer and proceed with our expedition, but, we must wait each week until there is a bus that has room on the roof to carry it.

The next Société Algérienne de Transports Tropicaux that would probably have room for our belongings and transport everything out of the Sahara into the French West African colony of Niger, was scheduled to depart in two weeks' time.

Desert vehicles were functional, but by no means beautiful. The driver's seat was raised high up to see over two radiators mounted on top of each other.

When ready to leave here for the journey to Agadez, the bus looked rough and ready with wares of all sorts stacked on the roof, hand luggage and water bags hanging around the exterior and passengers crammed inside with turbaned heads leaning out of bare window frames. With our trailer on board, we came away wondering if we would ever see it again!

During our short stay here, we walked to the camel market. There were pack camels, riding camels and a few runner camels for sportsmen who liked to race them. Camels have a prominent part in the lives of desert people and even today in the age of our super-trucks and helicopters or motorcycles, the camel is still the most satisfactory means of transport across sand.

When a camel caravan that may have been travelling twenty-five miles a day for ten days, without food or water, transporting their precious 350,000lbs of commodities such as salt, grain, sugar and almost everything for human survival, arrived at an oasis, there was considerable activity.

One mile south of the market place, camel tracks from the West (Timbuktu); the East (Bilma); the North (Ghardaia) and the South (Agadez) intersected in the desert sands making Tamanrhasset the crossroads of the Sahara. A friendly Arab lowered two camels down to their knees for Blenk and me to mount and ride. The leather rein which the guide put in my left hand, went under the neck from a ring through its right nostril. He put my feet cross-ankled in the curve of its soft hairy neck, then made it ungracefully lurch, without me falling off, to get up its hind legs first. With each lilt or movement of its walking stride, my feet would goad or prod the neck as it went along. Somehow I could sense the camel knew I didn't know how to ride!

While we were in the Hoggar Massif we had peeked at a lifestyle that been going on for centuries. In convoy, a rope from the camel's nose-ring is tied to the saddle of the one in front, so fastening forty or so camels together in a 'string'. Often as many as thirty strings, amounting to 1,200 beasts of burden came all together in single file, stretching out a very long way back to make up a caravan. Two people ride in seats slung across its back, being about the same weight, give or take a few pounds, as a load carried in convoy. If a camel is not well trained, it can be very stubborn and nasty, kicking or biting and becoming quite dangerous with no liking for its master. An Arab or Tuareg, wrapped in a flowing garment, is sometimes not easily recognized, even by his own friends, but can be singled out by his camel and the way he rides. The saddle has a rounded seat with a high shaped pommel in the design of the Tuareg symbol, a 'Croix du Sud' – the constellation of the Southern Cross.

In the market place, booths were scattered around. At each stage of our journey the price of food and fuel became more expensive. Packaged food and processed nutrition were unheard of in those days, so we bought dates, jam, powdered milk and, like natives, fed off the land. Bread was our staple food. Flour to make our bread had to be obtained from the quartermaster in charge of supplies and taken to the local baker. Blenk had no idea how much flour was needed for a loaf of bread and I did not know how much bread could be made from a kilo of flour! We had to convert our British shillings and ounces into French francs and kilos. On scraps of paper we estimated the amount of flour to buy to make enough bread for two of us for six days. The cheerful man selling it spoke Arabic and Hausa, but could not understand our figures because it was a bigger order than usual. He checked the figures and the quantity, but no one could agree about weight, quantity or price. At last calculations came close and we bought four kilograms of the flour to take to the baker who said our bread would be ready on the day we were to leave. Meanwhile, we had other things to do.

The next morning two mounted Legionnaires leading two harnessed horses, each mounted with native trim and decorative trappings, courtesy of the Captain, came trotting along the palm-lined way to our shelter. They had come to take us for a ride beyond the oasis and to gallop over the sand. The Legionnaires, wearing typical *kepi* head-dress, sat astride these 'drinkers of the wind', were silhouetted against the blue sky, resembling character heroes in a movie. The wind blew the tails of the horses sideways, just as it had lashed us up on the Tademait plateau, a few days ago. Riding horseback in the Sahara with the French Foreign Legion made amends for the hardships we had endured to reach here. It was another highlight of our expedition to be remembered.

The personnel stationed at outposts in the Sahara were extraordinary individuals. They were Legionnaires of regiments of the French Foreign Legion. The Legion is a voluntary army of a relatively small, closely united company of soldiers and is perhaps the most interesting military force in the world. A recruit of any nationality is not required to give his real name, or age. His enlistment is accepted with no questions asked. An applicant must join on French soil, be physically fit and make an oath first and foremost that he will be loyal to the Legion for a term of five years. The saga behind that pledge is of a Legion that offers home to any man in the world – who is unfortunately an outcast, for whatever reason, whether military, political, social or economic sufferer, or even a criminal. The regiment provides the ultimate life for a broken soul or an adventurous and brave spirit. The unit has served in the austere territory of North Africa for many years to subdue Moslem uprisings in Algeria and tribal raids on camel caravans to keep trade routes open, safe-guarding wireless installations at each oasis and taking care of search and rescue missions such as our breakdown contract.

The Captain invited us to his residence for dinner one evening before leaving and once again we enjoyed a touch of civilized living. Officers in his regiment of the French Foreign Legion, whose duties were much the same as personnel at other outposts, were introduced in order of rank: Lieutenants, wireless operator, medic, cook and two new *fonctionnaires* who were quite mystified by the two *jeunes femmes* travellers.

We were all seated around the long table arranged in lovely French style down the centre of the dining room. A well groomed Arab orderly on duty, in white uniform wearing a scarlet sash, stood behind the Captain's chair waiting to serve the meal. In a soft voice the Captain lowered his head and Blenk and me, in respect lowered our heads, but after a while of not being able to understand a word in French wondered what was being said for so long! We enjoyed a delightful, by comparison with our trek fare, *repas* of roast goat, fresh vegetables, canned peaches, delicious French pastries, red wine and good company.

Back at the desert garage, after a few days' rest, we prepared our kit for the next part of the Sahara trek to Agadez, the last oasis. By the regrettable process of elimination, everything except life-support items had to remain here in the trailer. Without the extra capacity of the trailer, we put aboard ten litres of fuel in the tank and carried three 20-litre containers of fuel in the sidecar for the single-cylinder Panther engine and the cooking stove. Food and water were geometrically wedged into place taking into consideration weight distribution. Oil for the Panther, unobtainable for two thousand miles, included two quart cans of very thick SAE 70 viscosity engine oil.

The well at In Guezzam, in the southern Erg Chech, two hundred and fifty miles or about half way to Agadez, had a desolate wireless outpost, but there would be no fuel or food available. Then briefcase, log book, passports and other impor-tant papers, were pushed in. We had now to forfeit comfort and protection and the other contents in the trailer for a while and came away from the SATT garage wondering if we would ever see our things again. Everything was ready . . . except the bread.

Bread was made daily. Bare loaves – no wrapping to keep it fresh and clean or preservatives to prevent it from getting hard and stale too soon. Late in the afternoon when we were due to depart, Blenk walked to the Bakery and returned shaking her head. 'Non! Not ready yet, *demoiselle*,' she said. Before sunset, I went off to the baker and on the way I watched a metal-worker using age-old bellows to puff up a fire while shaping a Southern Cross. I very much wanted a souvenir to remind me of the Tuaregs and glorious desert nights under the constellation of the Southern Cross, but sadly I did not buy it as all non-essential items had to be omitted from our gear. I walked back to the shelter shaking my head at Blenk saying '. . . *pas fini* – not ready yet'.

Early the next morning, on the day of our departure, Blenk tramped over there again and soon came stomping back as she could not understand what had happened. 'You!', she blamed me, 'you got the decimal point in the wrong place'. She went on, 'there is ten times too much bread' and, in the same breath, 'all the shelves are filled – the whole place is full of bread!' She continued, 'I asked which is ours. He turned with outstretched arms indicating all of it!' 'Wal,' she said, 'he must have been baking all night with enough flour to feed a tribe. You've bought enough bread to last us to Cape Town!' All the bread was tightly packed in by splitting loaves into small pieces to fill in the gaps. The Captain stipulated a six-day time allowance under the breakdown contract for us to reach the wireless outpost at In Guezzam.

At daybreak, on 18th January 1935, on- and off-duty soliders were at the rest station to bid us 'Adieu!' I glanced back to wave good-bye and have a last look at the Saharan refuge as we rode away with ends of the long French bread sticking up here and there, smelling like a *boulangerie*.

Steering into the blue, or I should say yellow, the bright dazzling glare from the vast expanse of yellow sand was so intense almost to lead to sun-blindness, and further squinting through tinted wrap-around glasses diminished our field of vision so much we could not always see clearly the ground ahead to avoid dangerous places. The sidecar wheel dropped into a hollow, but without the trailer to steady it, we tipped sideways with the

Panther lying over the sidecar. Fortunately no harm was done, no water had spilled and only a few drops of fuel leaked from the tank's filler cap. We gathered up our scattered belongings and carried on as if nothing had happened.

Down the Hoggar Massif, descending 1,000ft, skimming over sand dunes like surfing sea waves, we grappled drifts with high revs in low gear. It was like tackling hazards in a club trials event. Chiding each other several times about intentionally picking out every rock and rift and nearly having us both fall off, we kept rolling along. We fell about three feet over an unseen rim that put a strain on every nut and bolt. Blenk on the 'Moseley' rear mudguard pillion seat, came down just right to hold on to something, saving herself from being dumped. Dark patches of hard mineral ground were showing up through the sand here and there and between them were these treacherous hollows of powder-like sand. We pounced from one hard patch to another to skim across these sand-traps until they became longer, deeper and softer and eventually trapped our wheels. Everything was unloaded again, carried across and then the unladen combination coaxed through these dangerous sink holes, while we sung the oarsman's chant, 'One – two – PUSH!'

The fuel we calculated using had not made allowance for actual engine running time when wheel-spinning, churning up the sand or zig-zagging to avoid very bad places. Besides, slow progress was taking up our breakdown contract allowance in temperatures ranging from 125 degrees Fahrenheit in the daytime to a chilly below 50 degrees Fahrenheit at night. All the while the Panther and ourselves worked harder, but our average speed decreased. Central Sahara is one of the hottest places on Earth in mid-summer. It seldom rains there and the hot ground would melt the soles off our shoes. Overland travel between these outposts would surely cease in time – hopefully, even at our snail's pace, we would still not be here by then!

In the rocky north, there were the *hammadas*, like the Tademait plateau; then the windswept *reg* area strewn with flint and sharp stones causing us numerous flat tyres. We crossed a *wadi*, a dried-up river bed, which was an obstacle all of its own, then in the bottom of great basins were the *ergs*, those vast puddles of sand in which we were now in the middle. We followed the line of least resistance southward towards In-Guezzam between rocks and sand drifts along a twisty course like that of a *wadi* where once upon a time a river may have flowed in different directions towards its destiny.

Our log book lost count of which day it was, or whether we slept or rode some nights, so we were unable to tell how much time remained on the breakdown contract to reach In-Guezzam and the wireless outpost.

The constellation of the Southern Cross appeared overhead as daylight faded beside a myriad other stars and we stopped to sleep, feeling that In-Guezzam was not far away. We had enough cocoa to add to the insipid water to make the night beverage and by now the bread was quite hard.

Little fussing to sit down and be comfortable on a nearby rock, I accidentally tipped over my mug of cocoa and it spilled. The sand drank it.

The sun came up anew the next morning. In a marvellous moment of surprise a light airplane appeared in the sky and swooped low overhead as if to dive in salute. Whether the plane was on a *Ligne du Hoggar* flight-path or a military reconnaissance mission we did not know, but its brief appearance boosted our spirits immensely, as we had not seen a living thing between the outposts where nothing lives, or can live – not even flies. A long time later, I found out that it was sent by a London weekly publication.

> The French military plane swooped low to examine the speck crawling slowly on through the illimitable burning wastes of the Sahara. Unbelievable sight. Two girls on a motorcycle and their equipment. With their precious load of petrol and still more precious water, they were travelling steadily south blazing a new trail to Nigeria. Hence through Equatorial Africa, taxing women and machine to the limit of endurance – to Nairobi and the all-red route to the Cape. Wonderful machine. Indomitable pair. Heroes of an achievement besides which every motorcycle record pales into insignificance.
>
> *The Motor Cycle*

Tired and weary, yet having to be alert as we neared In-Guezzam, both of us were very much on the lookout for any trace of habitation or sign of life. The rider was the close-up spotter seeking to avoid or negotiate hazardous places, while the pillion passenger was the long-range observer. Heat haze made things visible, then vanish. Was it another mirage? Wind had blown sand heaped against the mud wall surrounding the tiny fort. Bare of palm trees, it was almost indiscernible in the distance, resembling a line of rocks along the ground and by not giving it enough attention, we nearly overlooked the place by-passing the fort entirely, which would have had disastrous consequences for us.

To prevent such a calamity from happening to any traveller, the Duty Sentry, standing on the mud roof, used a primitive method to signal us by using two mirrors (a heliograph) to converge brilliant beams of sunlight to flicker them on us and attract our attention. Suddenly it became a moment of joy. We had been contacted! Yes, there it was, In-Guezzam. We could now actually see the wireless masts and altered our course slightly westward and steered towards the fort.

We had crossed the Grand Erg Occidental, as this region was known, with little search-and-rescue time, fuel or water to spare.

At the gate in the mud wall surrounding the wireless outpost, the operator stood ready to meet us with a broad grin on his face and with a hearty handshake, he shouted, 'Bravo ... BRAVO!' At that moment, as fate would have it, the rear tyre had yet another puncture.

ALBERTO GRANADO

Extract from

TRAVELLING WITH CHE GUEVARA: THE MAKING OF A REVOLUTIONARY

Alberto Granado was born in 1922 in Cordoba, Argentina. In 1952 he and his friend and fellow medical student, Ernesto 'Che' Guevara (fondly known as Fúser or Pelao), embarked upon an exploration of South America on Alberto's 500cc Norton, nicknamed La Poderosa II (the Mighty One). The trip was Alberto's idea and came from a desire not only to travel and explore but also to experience and understand the people of their continent and their lives. The Norton only lasted until Chile but the journey was to change both men for ever. Each man kept a diary, both of which were subsequently published; Guevara's in 1967 and Granado's in 1978.

Alberto moved to Cuba and was to become Professor of Medical Biochemistry in the Faculty of Medicine at the University of Havana in 1961.

He died in March 2011 aged 88.

More calamities:
volunteer firemen
Los Ángeles, 27 February 1952

Here we are in the Los Ángeles Volunteer Firemen's barracks. How did we get here? Fate. I'll go back to the 21st.

Once we'd recovered from the knock, we managed to get to Lautaro. There, after a series of diplomatic manoeuvres – and against my better judgement – we decided to get the gearbox welded. It took two days and cost us the last of our cash.

The first day, we were invited to lunch by a petrol-pump attendant from the garage where we left the bike. He's a German who used to live in Paraguay and then settled in Chile. He has a married daughter in Sarandí, in the province of Buenos Aires, and wanted us as an audience – provided all he heard was praise for Argentina. We were delighted.

That night we met up with a crowd of Chileans who were just like the crowd back home. There was the storyteller, the Casanova, one who was the butt of every heavy-handed joke, the tightwad and the spendthrift – in other words, these small towns are just like any small town in Argentina.

We got on with them, and they offered us some wine. We accepted, and after a few glasses we all decided to go to a dance on the wrong side of the tracks. The dance hall was a building on the edge of town. A number of cars and lorries, parked every which way round a dim single-storey building, told us this was the place.

We went in and were welcomed by a blast of smoke reeking of alcohol and blended with that unmistakable odour of sweat winning out over perfume. A few drunken couples were dancing to something vaguely resembling a tango. But most of the public was crushed round a zinc counter, where alcoholic drinks – mainly wine – were sold.

We soon met a few familiar faces: a couple of farm hands who had helped us get our broken bike back on the road, and another who, while we waited, had given us a recital on the *charango*, an instrument made out of the shell of an armadillo. There was also a group of drunks who – thanks to the booze and the tangos – instantly became our nearest and dearest friends.

It wasn't long before the wife of one of them took a fancy to Pelao. Despite his grimy overalls and less-than-aesthetic stubble, being a foreigner and quite good-looking made him coveted prey.

I was already dancing with an Indian woman who was very fond of Argentines and the tango, but who, despite her tastes, wasn't doing much to lead me on. I was thinking about man's capacity to adapt and about his sensory apparatus, when a sudden commotion shook me out of my philosophical musings. The centre of attention was Ernesto, who – excited by the atmosphere and the drink – had tried to drag his devoted admirer outside.

She had been agreeable at first, but suddenly changed her mind and began shouting. Her husband came over immediately, armed with a bottle, and was about to hit Fúser from behind. When I saw what was going on, I dropped my partner, ran over to the man and grabbed him from behind. I floored him, or rather – thanks more to the wine than my blow – he fell. Taking advantage of the confusion, I fled after Pelao, who was already on the run. A few minutes later, back in our room and still gasping for breath, Fúser said, 'If we go to any more of these dances, we must solemnly promise not to sweep the women off their feet.'

With the exception of the above-mentioned episode, our two days in Lautaro were boring and we spent the whole time dealing with the bike. When we left, the petrol-pump attendant organised a farewell lunch for us in the company of several neighbourhood girls. They were all very affectionate. Once again I noted the greater freedom of Chilean women. The prudishness of the Argentine middle class in keeping an eye on their daughters doesn't exist here. We left after the meal.

A few miles further on we had another mishap, and I again witnessed Ernesto's level-headedness and quick reactions. Once past the built-up area, where I always drive because I'm the one with the international licence, I turned the bike over to Fúser. As we rounded a bend we ran into a drove of oxen, and I heard Ernesto call out in a slightly shaky voice, 'The brake's gone!'

We were going downhill and we could see that the slope ended in a row of poplars some 400 yards ahead. The bike was still picking up speed, but in fact I felt no fear. Looking back on it now, knowing that a river ran behind the poplars, I reckon this could have been the end of the line for us. At the very least we might have broken a few bones. But all I did was tell Fúser to brake using the gears and run the bike into the hill.

With a degree of confidence quite unwarranted in an in-experienced driver, Ernesto got the bike into third, then into second, which reduced our speed considerably, and finally, with difficulty, he got it into first. At once, taking advantage of our slower speed, he aimed the bike straight at the bank. As I jumped off the back he spread his legs, and I saw him come off the seat just a fraction of a second before the front wheel hit the mountain. We ran to switch off the engine to prevent a fire, and then shook hands, happy still to be alive.

What had happened was bound to happen. The thread of the wing nut that held the brake lever in place had completely worn away, and the nut had come off. We made our way back to a smallholding we had seen a minute or two before. They gave us some wing nuts that we used to patch up the lever, and two hours later we were on our way again.

Owing to our having patched up the gearbox, the bike began to lose power, and as night was coming on we asked for shelter at an *hijuela*, the local name for a parcel of land smaller than a smallholding. We were offered a place in the straw loft. But as the Temuco daily paper had got there ahead of us, one of the owner's daughters knew who we were and whispered something to her father, thanks to which we were invited to dinner. Then they put us up in the guest room.

The next day they gave us a magnificent breakfast, and we left firmly convinced that the press really is the fourth power in a bourgeois republic and that a lot of people believe more in the printed word than in what they see with their own eyes. How dangerous such power can be in unscrupulous hands!

On we went, now struggling against the bike itself as well as the road. Plagued by the strange noises it was making, we stopped at midday on a side-road shaded by chestnut trees. There we stripped down the clutch and adjusted the central wing-nut.

With the bike running a little better, we started up the hill by the River Malleco, which is spanned by the highest railway bridge in all of South América. Halfway up, the chain snapped. We had to stop right there since we didn't have a spare.

We managed to get a lorry driver to give us a lift as far as the little town of Culli Pulli, where a blacksmith was able to mend the chain, but night surprised us in this flurry of activity. A young man who lived nearby offered us a place to sleep, but in exchange we had to listen to a series of tales in which he was either a witness or a protagonist. In each of them there was always at least one dead body.

The next day we tried to carry on, but it was impossible. 'Poderosa II' was begging for mercy. We decided to wait for some new lorry to give us a lift, which didn't take long. As we drove along we felt a growing desire to leave the bike behind in Santiago de Chile and make our way to Caracas as best we could. I think this way we'd see more and be freer, and we'd be rid of the romantic air of continent-crossing bikers that surrounds us and distorts our view of reality.

The lorry took us as far as Melleco. There we made another attempt to continue by bike, but as 'Poderosa' was making ever louder and stranger noises, we decided to stop and ask for help from lorry drivers, that long-suffering guild, who have helped us more than anyone.

While we waited, Fúser made maté and, as ever, the familiar taste combined with the beauty of the landscape inspired me to review everything we'd seen so far in Chile – the beauty of the Andes, the smallholdings golden with wheat, the rich orchards dripping with apples and pears. And in contrast, the down-trodden *huasos*, poorly dressed in their unfailing ponchos and frayed, wide-brimmed hats, on small horses as famished as the riders themselves, who turn to drink in an attempt to escape their poverty. I also thought of the typical foreman, who fills in for his absentee master and is repellent even in the way he dresses – like an off-duty matador, in a pinched, short black jacket, trousers tight down to the ankles, a tilted hard-brimmed hat and short boots adorned with huge spurs. This is the man who speaks ill of his farm hands, calling them drunkards and slackers, and does nothing to improve their lot. Instead, he thinks he's doing himself a favour by singing the boss's praises, without realising that he's betraying himself and his class.

Suddenly a lorry turned up and interrupted my ruminations. We hoisted up the poor old bike and went back to Los Ángeles. After a bit of negotiating, we found ourselves at the police headquarters talking to a couple of sergeants who'd been stationed on the Argentine border, where they had been fêted and wanted to repay the attention by inviting us home. On our way, they kept up their panegyrics in praise of Argentine hospitality, and as the way was long and the story short they repeated it over and over – each time enriching it and becoming more and more moved by their own tale.

Unfortunately the lady of the house did not feel the same enthusiasm for Argentines as her husband, and that night we went to bed with sorrow in our hearts and nothing in our bellies.

Los Ángeles, 28 February 1952

Last night we had one of the wildest and most interesting adventures of our trip. During the day we made friends with two girls who seemed interested in getting to know us. Soon we were on good terms and they introduced us to the head of the town's volunteer fire brigade. With the girls' support we persuaded him to let us spend the night where they keep the fire engines.

After dinner we went out with the girls. Once again we found a marked difference between the attitudes of women in Chile and in Argentina with regard to the opposite sex. Perhaps the fact that we are 'birds of passage' makes things more possible, but I think the difference lies in their upbringing.

We ambled back to the fire station in silence, chewing over our respective experiences. The place where we were to sleep was narrow, with a slit for a window, and Fúser lay down beside it. He was in a state of agitation, but whether because of his asthma or the girl, I don't know. I tossed and turned in my sleeping bag, and when I got up for the umpteenth time I found a tiny stairway that led up to the roof. Climbing, I found myself in a kind of cupola, open on all four sides. It was cold, but I curled up in my sleeping bag and fell asleep.

I don't know how much time went by, but I was woken by a noise so deafening I felt my eardrums splitting. Leaping up, I felt a rope brushing my shoulder. It was the pull attached to the clapper of the fire bell. I had lain down to sleep right under the bell, just a couple of feet below it. The din and the vibrations were atrocious.

I hurled myself down the stairs to find Pelao already talking with the night watchman and asking him to let us help. The fire chief arrived and lent us a couple of helmets and protective jackets. Moments later we were racing along, clinging to the side of a fire engine called Chile-España.

After a mile or so we began to make out the glow of the flames, and then the typical smell of burnt resin you always get with conifers. In spite of the way we all pitched in, the building, which was made of pine timber and reeds, was almost completely destroyed. One group went at the brush fire that extended into the woods, while the rest of us attacked the house and an outbuilding.

I worked on one of the hoses, and Fúser removed the debris. When the blaze was under control, we heard the meowing of a cat trapped in the smoking remains of the roof.

Fúser went to look for it in spite of the protests of the other firemen, who wanted to get back to their beds. But when Fúser came back with the kitten in his hands everyone applauded, and they decided to keep it as the station mascot.

On our way back we remarked on the chances that on our first night in Los Ángeles we should witness and help to fight a fire, but the explanation was simple enough. In this wooded area, there are almost 400 fires a year – some caused by accident, some by carelessness, and some by landowners who burn the woods to grow crops. So there are fires almost every day and sometimes two or three. The next day we were given pennants as souvenirs of our participation.

Santiago de Chile, 1 March 1952

In Los Ángeles we made contact with a lorry driver who was moving furniture to Santiago. He charged us 400 Chilean pesos to carry our bike and took us on as porters for 50 pesos plus meals.

We bade farewell to our friends at the fire station, had a somewhat more affectionate send-off from the girls and set out for Santiago.

We reached the capital on Saturday. My first impression was that I was back in Córdoba, though the mountains here are

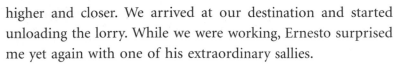

higher and closer. We arrived at our destination and started unloading the lorry. While we were working, Ernesto surprised me yet again with one of his extraordinary sallies.

As a joke we began to praise the strength of the lorry driver's mate, who, to show off how tough he was, began unloading the heaviest pieces. The owner was watching us, and he started making sarcastic remarks about Argentines, saying we were all weedy and slackers. Fúser and I gave as good as we got. Little by little the lorry driver lost his temper, and when he ran out of clichés to counter our banter he came on as the big boss. 'Right, you two can carry that wardrobe,' he told us. 'That's what I hired you for.'

The wardrobe in question was a vast piece of furniture made of extremely heavy wood, and it barely fitted through the narrow hallway. Ernesto and I were trying to manoeuvre it into position, but without much success. The driver's mate came to give us a hand, but his boss stopped him, saying, 'Hold it right there, José. Let the lads from Buenos Aires manage on their own.'

Pelao turned, looked the boss in the eye and said, 'Look what I can do if I've a mind to.' And turning to me, he added, 'Mial, you stay out of this.' Putting his arms round the wardrobe, he lifted it about four inches off the ground, carried it along the hallway and left it in the middle of the bedroom. Then he came back to where the three of us stood, dumbstruck by his perform-ance, and announced, 'That's me done.' And he sat down on the kerb beside the bike. I don't know where he found the strength to do what he did.

When we finished the job we took the bike to the workshop of an Argentine who lives in Chile. Then we went to the Argentine embassy to look for mail. There we met the consul, another candidate for our collection of shameless characters. He wanted us to believe he suffered from an occupational disease owing to the quantity of drink he had been obliged to consume at official functions. This had given him a gastric ulcer that he claimed would send him to the grave. Since he drinks like a fish, I think he'll be carried off by delirium tremens.

PATRICK SYMMES

Extract from

CHASING CHE

Patrick Symmes is a writer, photographer and journalist who has contributed articles to many publications including the *New York Times*, *Daily Telegraph*, *Newsweek*, *Harper's* and *Condé Nast Traveler*. His expertise lies in South and Latin America, particularly Cuba.

In 1996 he sought to recreate the classic motorcycle journey taken by Ernesto 'Che' Guevara and his friend Alberto Granado in 1952. He travelled through Argentina, Chile, Peru and Bolivia on a BMW R80GS trying to see the places and meet those characters that helped to influence and mould the man who was to become the most iconic and charismatic revolutionary of the twentieth century.

There are moments on a motorcycle when all the glory of motion is distilled into one purposeful package. Chasing curves over a swelling landscape, a motorcycle enters the pure expression of physics and is bound to the road in a way no car will ever know. The rider and machine are literally balanced on the infinitely thin line where centripetal forces meet gravity. Despite this state of suspended disaster, the sensation of risk is largely a sensation; the motorcycle is in harmony with the road, and risk comes overwhelmingly from other drivers. Any moment of travel on a motorcycle is a light and essential moment, an agile rebuke to a life conducted in one place. The raw force of the engine is not hidden beneath a hood, but alternately purrs and growls a few inches from the knees, demanding the consciousness of power. Sealed behind glass, insulated by climate control systems and music, the driver of a car knows nothing about the directions of the wind, the lay of sunlight, the small changes in temperature between a peak and a valley, the textured noise of differing asphalts, or the sweet and sour aromas of manured fields or passing pine forests. Engaged in all the senses and elements, balanced in the present tense, a rider on two wheels can taste moments of oneness with the road.

Alas, this wasn't one of those moments. After three hard days and two bad nights I came finally to a sliding, squirming halt in a thick pebbly gravel at the end of Valdés Peninsula. The truck driver had been right. I was on my own.

National Route 3, as the road south was called, had been pockmarked, scarred, and prone to sudden fits of gravel, all in all a merciless experiment in moving fast down a dangerous yet utterly boring route that lasted hour after hour, morning and afternoon, day after day, interrupted only by brief interludes in hideous gas stations manned by surly men dishing overpriced fuel. This shakedown cruise was pure pain: the new Plexiglass windscreen on the bike proved too short by a few inches, so that a sixty-five-mile-an-hour wind slipped over the top and tugged at my helmet all day, pressing the chin strap into my neck; the tip of my nose burned red and then peeled; my shoulders and behind complained incessantly; I became very dirty. Later I would miss the Ruta Nacional 3, of course, but I didn't know that at the time.

Patagonia is immense and more impressive than lovely in its austere vastness. With every mile south the land turned a lighter brown. Green grasses faded to tan clumps on a canvas of powdery soil. Where the road cut near the sea I saw a churlish and black Atlantic dressed with constant whitecaps. It was an ever-diminishing landscape: flatter, emptier, windier, a desert without sand, hot by day and cold by night. The last hundred miles out from the peninsula were on a loose gravel track that caught the wheels and threw me down twice. I'd topped up my tank in the pathetic town where the gravel began, and each time the bike fell over gasoline trickled out of the carburetors, wetting the stones. The dark stains evaporated quickly in a wind that ripped off the Atlantic at twenty-five miles an hour, an offshore blast that smelled only of fathomless distance, of the great expanse of ocean east toward Africa and south toward the ice.

Valdés Peninsula is a geologic oddity, thrust far into the cold currents of the South Atlantic yet home to the lowest point in South America, a broad, white salt pan some thirty-five metres below sea level that I had passed quickly on my way in. This featureless plain was the dullest tourist site I'd ever seen, but every day a bus pulled to a halt beside it, disgorging groups of visitors who were expecting the Patagonia of wall calendars. The buses progressed around the peninsula, pausing at ocean vistas and heading always to the north point, where, if you arrived at high tide, you might see one of the local orcas charge the beach, scattering—and only occasionally catching—the seal pups that played tauntingly in the surf. The rest of the peninsula was satisfyingly empty, a landscape without utility poles or houses or pavement.

I'd finally come to a halt at Caleta Gonzalo, a zipper of a bay at the ocean end of the hundred-mile peninsula. Twice a day, Caleta Gonzalo opened along its length and closed again, breathing water in and out in an enormous tidal swing that exposed almost ten miles of mud, then reflooded it. Steep cliffs dropped down to a beach where a dozen obese sea elephants brayed and dozed. Despite the briny stink of the tidal flats, the beach looked attractive. I'd driven back and forth for miles, scaring up a rare Patagonian fox and several loping *guanacos* but failing to spot even a single dip or hollow to shield my tent from the wind, nor any man-made structure to provide lee shelter. From on high you could spy the magellanic penguins as they waded into the water and fell over with a cute belly flop. In an instant these waddling land creatures were reborn as subsurface birds, their useless wings now fins that helped them school in speedy flocks through the undersea.

Everywhere, the elements sounded their warnings. A

blood-orange light fled the setting of the sun behind me, and the wind already carried a premonition of how cold it would be in half an hour. I needed shelter quickly. Night was minutes away, and in this unpopulated zone I was ready to ignore the No Camping signs sprinkled thoughtfully along the cliff, but I knew why they were really there. At high tide the beach would disappear, and the water came in like a flash flood. If you were asleep on the beach you would never make it. A month before my arrival a careless camper had been killed that way.

I drove south on the bay road, rounding bluff after bluff in search of any sheltered spot, but the ground was flat everywhere and scoured by the violence of the air. If I'd had a car I could have slept in it, but instead I needed protection from elements that cared nothing for 'oneness.'

Hurrying along, I almost passed a little farm nestled in a dell where the cliffs briefly faded away and a cluster of buildings touched the high-water line. There were four sheep ranches on the Valdés Peninsula, and these buildings were an outstation on the biggest, which ran more than 40,000 head.

This is where my filth came in handy. If there was one thing I was learning to admire about the young Ernesto Guevara, it was his unmitigated gall. As story after story in his diary showed, the man was absolutely shameless, master at the traveler's art of scamming, borrowing, begging, or otherwise landing accommodation, favours, food, clothes, money, introductions, jobs, dance partners, and liquor. When it came to freeloading, Guevara was a prince. 'We aren't that broke,' he once wrote to his mother after cadging a bed in a hospital, 'but explorers of our stature would rather die than pay for the bourgeois comfort of a hostel.'

Menaced on both sides by barking black dogs, I rode down the driveway of a ranch, dismounted, and clapped twice. Then

I waited the customary two minutes, the black dogs barking all the while, circling slowly as I stood stock still. I spent the time preparing a little speech. I had to sound needy, yet not desperate. I had to plead for a roof, neither so demanding that I would offend nor so tentative that I would be rejected. I had to balance a humble tone with the subtle implication that I was a person of enormous importance, deserving of aid. For proof of the latter, I carried in my breast pocket a letter of introduction from a New York magazine, ready to spring forth like a passport from the Other World.

When he came out—a fat, greasy fellow in a sun-bleached PARIS ELLE t-shirt, his hair wild in the wind—he didn't wait for my speech. He looked at the setting sun, the distant horizon, and above all the dirt on my clothes.

'Come in, come in,' he said, 'you had better spend the night.' His name was Florio, and he had the buttery handshake of a man who handled sheep. He waved at the dogs, who fell silent, and led me inside.

My bed was the floor of the cookhouse. After three twelve-hour days of riding my ugly cockroach of a motorcycle, I slept soundly and long. The broken cement felt like a down mattress.

The hens woke me when they strutted into the shed and bobbed nervously, emitting feed-me clucks. The tin roof played a twangy tune, like an instrument in the wind that had risen during the night. Outside it was blowing hard enough to send an unhappy hen rolling beak-over-talon past the shed from time to time.

Florio listened to the radio, measured the wind, and sent his son David out to tell me that I was grounded. It was gusting to forty-five miles an hour and I could not drive. The boy told me this and kept talking. The dam of solitude first leaked and then gushed. Nine years old, living in isolation with his father and 40,000 sheep, the boy needed nothing so much as to speak. As I stood silently with him in the sunshine, both of us leaning against the wind, he unleashed everything at once, a gale of words about the neighbours, who lived an hour away, and the level of water in the well, which was low, and the whales and sharks which came into the bay. He named the starving cats that wandered the yard eyeing the chickens, and explained the work histories of both black dogs, along with the good qualities of various birds, the murderous nature of foxes, and which of every animal that walked or swam was good or bad, which cherished or hated. He talked of the orcas that came into the bay to hunt seals and tasty sea lion pups, and of the tourists who came on great lumbering buses to watch the orcas hunt, and of the water truck, which was three days late, and of the strange English boy he met once at a boarding school, a boy who spoke very oddly, almost as though he had different words for things.

'*Myaw myaw myaw*; we couldn't understand anything he said,' David explained. The fever or speech ran on, burning at the boy so badly that he twitched and jumped and jumbled words, hunching down to tell me about the colouration of chicken eggs, then jumping up to describe the stars we would see at night, and the paths of air-planes, and the cost of soccer balls, and his fervent desire to drink Coca-Cola. 'I go through mountains of shoes my father says I'm crazy he can't believe it but I don't do anything except when it's raining and the mud gets everywhere and the rain kills the chickens that one lays white eggs it's the only one the *patrón* comes to visit sometimes and I showed him but if it's an east wind it's cold and wet and that kills the chickens or the fox comes and gets them which is why they sit in their bush all night where the dogs don't chase them I like the cats better my kitten is better will you take a picture of him?'

By my watch he talked for twenty-five minutes without interruption. What finally stopped him was that I belched, and at this he fell over in the dirt and chicken shit and began laughing his head off, the fever of an entire solitary winter broken by a fit of endless giggles. He'd never heard a foreigner belch before. Before he could start talking again, I asked him if he'd ever heard of Che Guevara.

David looked broken by my question. My tone told him it was an adult matter, something serious and from the outside world, but I was mouthing words as meaningless as those of the strange little English boy at boarding school. This was something from beyond the realm of foxes and sea elephant pups and good and bad winds. 'Does he play football' he asked tentatively.

Later I risked the short trip to the north shore, but the orcas never came and the seals sunned themselves unmolested. When I got back Florio was still sitting inside at the same table, his ear tuned to the transistor voice of the world. There was no news from the atmosphere.

In the morning I lay on the floor listening to the roof, which struck a lower tone than the day before. The shed was decorated with old shears and handmade knives hanging from the wall, their rusty points dangling down in the general direction of my sleeping bag. The tools were waiting for October, for the 40,000 sheep to finish converting grass into wool and then to line up in the chutes and paddocks and march in steady panic under these sharpened edges.

Little David came to the door carrying the same message from his father that I had heard in the tin roof: the wind was down in the twenties. David stood just inside the doorway of the cook shed, silent but clearly crestfallen by my decision to abandon him to the sheep and cats and chickens and orcas. He watched with wide eyes as I handled each of my possessions in turn, brushing stray down from my sleeping bag and stuffing it away, nestling my tiny cook stove in a saddlebag, dropping my flashlight into the zippered tank bag that would fit on the bike between my knees, one piece of kit after another. You could carry a lot if you packed carefully.

'This is the airplane that brought you here,' he said. I turned and saw he was pointing at one of the last things I packed, the book of outdated hotel listings and dubious restaurant recommendations that were supposed to be guiding me across South America. It lay open to the very first page, an advertisement for SAETA, the Ecuadorean airline. Like all airline ads it showed a clean jet rising up in a blue sky. I told David that I had come on a different airplane.

'From where?' he said. I turned to the map of Argentina in the guidebook and showed him the Valdés Peninsula and how it lay far to the south of Buenos Aires.

'Is Buenos Aires in your country?'

This was serious. I unpacked my big map of South America and explained that Buenos Aires was in his country, while mine lay still further to the north. He pointed to the north of Argentina: 'Here?' Farther north, I replied. He looked slightly defeated by the news that there was more than one airplane, but I gave him a set of batteries for his transistor radio, which had died months ago. Now, like his father, he could have a one-way conversation with the world. I said good-bye to Florio, who looked relieved to see me go and asked that I send David a book, which I did.

Driving out the peninsula, the wind knocked me over twice more, sending me into knee-scraping mounds of pebbles. When the bike blew over the second time the windshield cracked. Gasoline leaked from the carburetors again; I watched the liquid evaporate from the stones in horror, quickly righting the bike each time but losing several pints that I could not afford to lose. Yesterday's trip to the north shore suddenly seemed a foolish waste of fuel. I hit the reserve tank with an hour still to go. Somehow I made it to the steep ridge of hills at the neck of the peninsula, but the motor began to cough and hesitate on the way up the last hill. I threw the petcock from *Res.* back to *Auf* and got one last burst of power that pushed me up to the crest at a wobbly five miles an hour. It was two paved miles from there to the gas station, but all downhill, and I eventually coasted into the little settlement of Puerto Pirámides like some pathetic bicyclist. I mailed a postcard to my girlfriend and bought a vanilla milk shade and a full tank of gas, and then sat on a chair on the beach drinking the milk shake, watching the tide surge right past the No Parking signs, up and over the legs of the chair, and while I sipped my milk shake the water ran forth and back beneath me, chilling the aluminium. I said over and over to no one in particular that this was a very fine town indeed. Six days, and already I was talking to myself.

ANDY MARTIN

CHE AND THE ART OF MOTORCYCLE MAINTENANCE

Andy Martin is the author of *Waiting for Bardot* and *The Boxer and the Goalkeeper: Sartre vs Camus* (2012). He teaches at Cambridge University while dreaming of 30-foot waves at Waimea Bay. He appears for a few tantalising seconds in the short, mysterious film *MML the Movie*.

should never have got rid of her. She needed a lot of strip-ping, but then she taught me everything I know about engines – the clutch, piston rings, and cylinder heads. Where is my old Francis-Barnett 'Cruiser' (249cc) now? More rusty than trusty, she used to start at least 50 per cent of the time, and there is something about that unpredictability that made her so much more endearing than the gleaming and reliable beast of a Honda 1000 that displaced her.

The death of Alberto Granado – Che Guevara's sidekick of *The Motorcycle Diaries* fame – brought it all back to me: the enchantment of the old motorbike, that can fly you like an angel across a continent – or plunge you into the depths of despair before you even get to the bottom of the road.

Especially the British bike, of course. Che and Alberto rode a dysfunctional Norton 500, ironically nicknamed 'La Poderosa II' ('The mighty one'). My father was a Velocette nut. I still have a photograph on my wall, going back to the 1930s, of the two young good-looking people who would eventually become my parents riding a Velocette somewhere on the Sussex coast and grinning their heads off. The bike was the symbol of liberation, even then.

If you were brought up in the mean streets of Upton Park in east London, then a bike was your passport to the great world of sun and sand and the wind in your hair (my father always hated to wear a helmet). For me it was a less a mode of transport than a way of not quite making it to school ('Sorry, sir, it's that Francis-Barnett again!').

For Che and Alberto revs and revolution were all one. Not only did the bike provide a convincing feeling of liberation as they rode across the countries of Latin America, like speeded up gauchos, leaving troubles behind them, but it brought them into contact with the proletariat every time it broke down and they had to seek out another mechanic. Or, to put it the other way around, Che always thought the revolution ought to be like a good bike, with the entire proletariat on the pillion, whisking them out of poverty and oppression in the general direction of the good life.

If only Che had stayed on his bike! After he was gunned down in the Bolivian jungles, Robert M. Pirsig pointed out, in his classic *Zen and the Art of Motorcycle Maintenance*, that you really ought to be able to fix your own bike. If you want to get from Minnesota to California, you shouldn't rely on mechanics, you have to get down and get dirty. If you can repair a carburettor then you should have no trouble at all saving your own soul. As Wittgenstein said, if you want to be philosopher, become a mechanic. Ultimately, you have to be the bike, as if you had Castrol running through your veins.

Obviously I was going to be a sucker for the *Easy Rider* style. The romance of the Harley choppers with the apehanger handle bars. The point about this bike was you had your legs stuck way out in front, like you were lying down. You were literally laid-back. It was always likely to end in tears, the journey across America. You could try to go coast to coast, but chances were you wouldn't make it, some vertical guys with pitchforks and shotguns living in Hicksville were bound to resent your freedom and try and drag you down. Let's face it, there is definitely an element of death-wish built into the motorbike. You have to enjoy the pain and the heartache. Better to go out with a bang than a phut.

Even though Alberto and Che and a whole generation of easy riders have gone up in exhaust smoke, the mystique of the long-distance biker lives on. A true nomad and wanderer on that endless ride into the sun, weaving in and out of lanes of gridlocked cars like a Brazilian winger going round plodding fullbacks. Two wheels good, four wheels bad.

DON WHILLANS

SOLO BY MOTOR-BICYCLE FROM RAWALPINDI TO LANCASHIRE

Don Whillans was born in Salford, Manchester in 1933.
He started on a career as a climber with his friend Joe
Brown in 1951. Abrasive, controversial, sometimes
unsavoury and yet totally unique, Whillans graduated from
rock-climbing to mountaineering and in 1970
triumphantly succeeded in making the first ascent of
Annapurna in the Himalayas. This extract recounts Don's
journey home to Lancashire on a 500cc Triumph from the
1960 expedition to conquer Trivor (25,370 ft) in the
Karakoram Himalaya led by Wilfrid Noyce.

A heavy drinker and smoker, Whillans acquired a
reputation for curmudgeonly confrontation and a life-long
problem with figures of authority but this archetypal
anti-hero was celebrated as an inspired mountaineer of
considerable skill and courage. He died of a heart attack
in 1985 aged 52.

On 24 September I was ready to start the 7,000-mile journey by motorbike from Rawalpindi to the U.K. After ten days' preparation I had got the necessary visa for Iran, and what was even more vital, some money. I was at last ready to leave the peace and quiet of Colonel Goodwin's house, and face six weeks of hard, hot and dusty driving through eight different countries. I said farewell to the Goodwins, and to the one remaining expedition member, Geoff Smith, and with good luck wishes ringing in my ears drove out on to the road to Peshawar, my first objective, 105 miles away.

I had first to make a call on an R.A.F. pilot I had met on the journey out by boat. He was stationed at Risalpar, a place just short of Peshawar. After three hours' drive, a signpost indicated a right turn, four miles to Risalpar. I soon found the camp and was directed to his quarters. Unable to attract any attention, I went to the bungalow next door, and an extremely attractive Pakistani girl informed me he had left for the weekend, and gone to Rawalpindi. After talking for some time she said that if I did not want to continue that day to Peshawar I would be quite welcome to stay the night with them. I did not take long to make up my mind. If I continued, I should probably end up at the Afghan border after dark and have no place to sleep. Later in the afternoon, her husband, a squadron leader in the Pakistan Air Force, returned, and fitted me out in more suitable dress for a drink in the mess.

In the evening conversation drifted to my plans for the journey home. I received many pitying glances from the company, as they began to fill me up with stories of murder and robbery in Afghanistan. The appearance of a missionary, much to my relief, put an end to the topic; and it came as no surprise to me later, as I had already discovered what a small world it is, to find that he lived only eight miles from my own home.

I retired to bed slightly uneasy, already imagining myself going flat out up the dreaded Khyber Pass, with bullets singing past my ears.

Next morning after a good breakfast, I loaded my belongings on the bike, and said good-bye to my hosts.

I was determined to spend the next night on Afghan soil. After I left Peshawar, the hills, through which the Khyber pass goes, soon appeared through the heat-haze of midday. As I approached the Pass, I thought of all the violence this place had seen, though it seemed fairly peaceable today. It wasn't long before I was stopped at a road block, with a couple of guards loaded down with bandoliers of bullets, to discourage any awkward customers from forcing a way through.

I was directed to a small hut at the side of the road and produced my passport.

'You have no frontier stamp,' I was informed. It seemed one had to report to the police at the last town and obtain a stamp on the passport in order to cross the frontier.

I drove back to Peshawar, and soon found the police station, closed! This seemed to be unusual, the police station closed, so after a careful search round the building, I discovered a side door open and a miserable fellow seated behind a desk. I produced the passport, and he disappeared into the chief office. One hour later I was heading back to the Khyber, a friendly nod at the road block, and I was entering the Pass on a good asphalt road, a thing I had hardly expected. Keeping a wary eye for snipers I stopped to take photographs and look at the badges of the many regiments cut into the rock. After passing several tribesmen with rifles walking along the road and not being shot at, I soon felt quite happy.

On arrival at the far end of the Pass I was halted at the Pakistan border. After a long business with papers I rolled up to the Afghan border 100 yards away. First they wanted the certificate of inoculation against cholera, as it seemed there was an epidemic on. After this the passport, *carnet*, etc. Everything seemed to have gone off all right, when I noticed a clerk looking very intently at my visa stamp. I guessed what was wrong: it had expired.

A few minutes later I was back on my way to Peshawar to book in at a hotel and wait for the Afghan Consulate to open office in the morning. By 9.30 next morning I had completed my calls on the Consulate and C.I.D. and was once more driving through the Pass, which by now seemed almost as familiar as the Llanberis Pass in Wales. This time everything went smoothly and in no time I was humming down the road towards Kabul, the capital of Afghanistan 180 miles away, very confident of reaching it before nightfall. For the first fifty miles to Jalalabad there is a super highway, and stories of Russian and American roads being built all over the country came to mind. Then came the rude awakening; this super highway was replaced by what I would call a farm track. What I did not know, as I began picking my way through the pot-holes and boulders, was that it was going to take me something like three and a half weeks' tough driving to reach the 'farm'. By 5 o'clock I had crashed the bike once, bent the footrest, and toppled it down a sand bank trying to avoid a lorry. I looked like someone out of a flour mill, and had a terrific thirst. I unpacked the primus stove and made two huge brews of tea, then fell asleep on the ground sheet.

I woke early, and continued towards Kabul through a very impressive gorge, through which the engineers were building a reasonable road, but unfortunately they hadn't made a lot of progress to date. I arrived in Kabul around 9.30, and stopped to watch the traders in the market. The best thing to do seemed to be to go to the British Embassy, where I would be able to get the information I required.

The Consul proved to be an extremely nice chap, and his assistant immediately offered me some breakfast, a wash, and a couple of bottles of beer to set me in the right spirits.

After breakfast I inquired about road conditions etc., and it seemed that I had arrived at the right time. The road I wished to travel on to Kandahar had just been opened that day; it had been closed because of the cholera epidemic. After the routine report to the police, I cashed some cheques in the bazaar and booked in at a reasonable hotel. By the time I had cleaned up in the shower, had a meal and the customary sleep in the afternoon, I discovered that I should be reporting to the Embassy for some more beer with the nice Consul.

After a very pleasant evening drinking and talking, I left the Embassy and discovered that the lights on the bike had failed. Having decided to accept the penalty for drunken driving without lights, I jumped on the machine and wove a course through the city back to my hotel and a clean bed.

After completing all necessary matters, like filling up with petrol and also the gallon can that I carried, I left Kabul wishing that I could have stayed longer. As the road might have closed again it was imperative to leave at the earliest opportunity. This

was the first really long stage of the journey, being 340 miles
with no cities in between. I drove all day, being stopped at several
road blocks and asked for my cholera certificate. The tightness
of the regulations regarding travel during an epidemic was beginning to cause me a little worry, for several reasons. First, cholera
inoculation needed two jabs and I had had only one; then, the
certificate had almost expired; and lastly, I might catch cholera.
Anyway luck held and by nightfall I had reached the halfway
stage. After a cup of tea and half a melon, a gift from the wagon
driver, I bedded down on the sand just off the roadside, only to
be awakened by the intense cold during the night.

The next day I expected to reach Kandahar, though I knew
I would be in for an extremely hard day. I was not disappointed;
for a solid ten hours I bounced along the track trying to stay
upright, sometimes in sand, at others in rock or gravel. Just
before darkness I had only 8 miles to go when I had the feeling
something had happened to the steering. A quick look revealed
a broken rear mudguard. Far too much weight, something would
have to go. It was too late to start to rearrange the packing, so
another night was spent in a dry river bed, the only disturbance
being caused by some animal rushing past my head just after I
turned in. The glimpse I had made me think it was a dog, or
could it have been a wolf? Not being sure if there were wolves
in Afghanistan I fell asleep still wondering.

After cocoa and a juggle with the kit I wobbled into Kandahar
in the early hours. Several essential jobs required attention, so I
decided to spend a couple of days in this city. After a clean-up
in the hotel I took the bike down to a welder in the bazaar and
had the mudguard repaired, then bought oil for the oil change
now due, and returned to the hotel. In the meantime, two girls
had arrived at the hotel, one from Oldham, some ten miles from

where I live, and a girl from New Zealand, travelling together back to England. We combined cooking arrangements and I enjoyed several good meals. Hotels in these countries do not object to cooking in the bedroom. Two bottles of beer arrived, one each for the girls from a chap down the corridor who appeared concerned for them, though I think he became even more concerned when I downed both bottles before he could say knife.

The following day I spent on routine maintenance of the bike and visits to various offices for stamps in the passport or on the certificate. During the evening several motorcycle dealers arrived, and began offering to buy the bike. Unfortunately there were too many technical snags, otherwise I would have sold the machine, their offers were very high and would have bought me a new machine with some to spare.

The next stage of 235 miles was reputedly the toughest, and so it proved to be, not that the road became any worse, but extremely hot and desolate; only towards evening, when nearing Farrah, did I see the odd village. There is one stopping place called Dilaram where one can buy petrol in tins if one is running short. Just as the sun began setting I pulled off the road and made camp for the night some 10 miles from Farrah.

A call in the bank next day proved unfruitful, they refused to cash a travellers' cheque. Stopping only long enough to buy a packet of cigarettes I pressed on to Herat, arriving around 4.30 p.m. I searched out a hotel and within minutes of my arrival had been invited to dine with a Swiss couple in the evening. He, it seemed, was a geologist, and had been in Afghanistan for several years. He asked if I had come through Dilaram, and told me he met the famous Peter Townsend there, while he was making his round-the-world trip. Also in the hotel were two

English lads travelling back from Calcutta and later my two ex-girl-friends from Kandahar arrived by bus.

The following day I carried out the usual routine of bank and garages in preparation for departure next morning.

I left early in anticipation of trouble at the frontier. I had been warned not to take food that had been opened as this would be thrown away by the Iranians at the border because of the cholera. The track became very sandy in places and I had great difficulty in crossing several troughs of sand. Mid-day saw my arrival at the frontier, the place seemed deserted. I eventually found the officers in charge asleep. They quickly clipped the necessary stamps, etc., and returned to their cots. A mile up the road I encountered the Iranian border post. They threw away my water and several bits of food, and checked my cholera slip for the last time, then I was heading for Kalla Islam, the frontier town. Here I encountered a whole host of people from the hotel in Herat. The last bus for the day had gone, so they were spending the night in a shed which was the town's hotel. I decided to stay the night and have a chat with the English-speaking people for a change, and spent the evening drinking Coca-Cola with an American who told me about the angry scene on the bus after one of the English girls discovered her camera had been stolen. Just when heads were about to roll a man cycled up and handed the camera over. How he came to have the camera in his possession was still a mystery.

On the journey from Kalla Islam I encountered my first bad 'corrugations' which in no time broke the mudguard again. My English friends passed me later in the day on the bus, waving, then disappeared in a cloud of dust, and that was the last I saw of them. I arrived in Meshed mid-afternoon, and after deciding one hotel was too expensive I tried the usual trick of picking on a knowing-looking youngster and repeating ''otel'. I was then taken through the town, and finished up at the same hotel. Tired out, I booked in, and after a shower and clean-up I had the mudguard welded; then set off to look around the famous 'Blue Mosque' and the bazaar.

Next day I picked up a student guide and made a tour of the city, buying several souvenirs, and a watch for £1 which I thought might just last the trip. It did, just! At Boulogne it packed up.

From Meshed to Teheran is 576 miles of horrible road; I expected to take three days for this leg of the journey. It did in fact take me four, and during these four days in the saddle many incidents occurred, some amusing, some not. At my first stop the entire police force arrived at my hotel in dribs and drabs until finally the chief himself arrived to see this stranger in the town. I was at first rather angry with all the town in my bedroom, particularly as I had the front wheel off the bike trying to repair a puncture. Later it became so comical during my interrogation, that I found it impossible to keep a straight face. Many severe glances were directed at me, which only added to my amusement. Finally with a stiff bow I was handed back my passport and the room was emptied.

The following mid-day found me seated by the roadside in a particularly deserted stretch with another puncture. Deciding that it was useless to use the same rubber solution again, I thought I would sit it out until someone arrived. Nightfall saw the wheel back on with the puncture repaired. Exhausted after my struggle all day in the sun, I slept at the scene of the mishap.

Deciding that the spare jerry-can of petrol was no longer necessary I threw it away, a good find for some wanderer. Pulling in at a small town for bread, I was immediately pounced on by the local bobby and while I was being once more interrogated, managed to have the mudguard welded again. At Damghan, my overnight stop in a cheap hotel, I traded a tin trunk for a decent job on my punctured tyre.

Ten solid hours' driving brought me to Teheran on the first stretch of tarmac road for weeks. The ride from Meshed had taken its toll of me. I looked a very sorry sight, dirty, unshaven, face badly cracked with weeks of exposure to the sun, and extremely sore. Deciding on a fresh start, I called the inevitable stray over and was guided to an expensive-looking hotel. The apartment was luxurious, own bathroom and telephone and all the trimmings. After a good bath and a huge meal I passed into oblivion between spotless white sheets.

Next morning, feeling much fitter, but around three pounds poorer, I visited the British Consulate to learn the dos and don'ts for leaving Iran. After taking the camera for repair, I visited a park to watch some tennis, quite a change in this part of the world. Nobody seems interested in wasting energy on sports of any kind.

From Teheran 100 miles of tarmac road were a marvellous change after the 'track'. However, all good things come to an end, earlier than usual around these parts, and soon the track re-appeared. While I was having a Coke in a transport café a G.B. Land Rover pulled in, the occupants being an Australian and an Englishman heading for England.

I put my kit in the Land Rover and we drove along together until nightfall, then camped in the desert for the night.

Leaving the two lads to repair the three flat tyres they had inherited overnight, I pushed on to the next town to await them and do some shopping. Whilst I was waiting for them, the London-Bombay bus pulled in, spilling a crowd of young people out and filling the village with the sound of Cockney voices. Talking to one fellow I asked him how he came to be going to India. 'Well I just got fed up, so I got on the bus at Hampstead Heath.' 'Got a job out there?' I asked, reminding him that there is no dole in India. 'No, I'll look around for a couple of weeks before I start work.' A few minutes later they were gone, leaving me scratching my head.

Meanwhile, the lads were having the patches vulcanized at a garage down the street. While strolling around, one particular 'nosy parker' who spoke a very few words of English began to annoy me. A fight looked like developing from the show I gave him, when I was informed that he was the chief of police, in civvies. After this I decided to leave town and drive slowly to allow the others to catch up. A mile from the town I stopped by a stream to swill the dust off the bike. About an hour later I saw the Land Rover approaching at a fast rate. I asked what the hurry was and they told me they had to make a run for it for refusing to pay the price asked by the garage man.

Later in the evening we arrived in Tabriz. A few inquiries soon had us installed in a reasonable hotel for the night. Next morning I said farewell to the boys, who wished to press on with all speed. The day was spent collecting exit permits and in changing money, also maintenance of the bike. The rear mudguard needed welding again. On the way to the welder's shop I had a head-on collision with a cyclist. In view of the threatening crowd, and the fact that I had been going up a one-way street, I had to pay up a pound and try to look happy.

The next day I expected to reach the borders of Turkey. I left at seven and drove steadily until mid-day when I caught up with two more Australians in a van. Over a thick slice of bread and jam we decided to press hard for the border, as we were all rather fed up with Iran and Iranians. The scene at the border post made us think of a hotel in Paris, quite luxurious and full of tourists. The fabulous cars made us think civilization had arrived.

True to form, trouble arrived in the shape of the passport officer, who went a little too far and began pushing people about. Unfortunately for him, none of us was in any mood, after a hard day, to be pushed about. He found himself in the unusual position of being an Iranian surrounded by a threatening crowd, and as this had never happened before he quickly disappeared into his office. It was too late to cross the frontier, so after a meal in the Tourist Hotel we slept in the yard on camp-beds.

Strangely enough it was our sparring partner from the previous evening who got us away one of the first in the morning. As soon as one entered Turkey there was a magnificent view of Mount Ararat, 16,900 ft. Seeing a snow-capped mountain after so much desert made me feel almost at home again. Although the roads were still unmetalled, there was a very marked improvement; also noticeable at once was the appearance of neat fields, and road signs. The most startling thing of all was that people were working. It was also nice to discover that the children didn't play the game of 'Stone the Motorcyclist' as in Afghanistan and Iran.

A few miles into Turkey we came across our old friends from Tabriz. Over breakfast the idea of climbing Mount Ararat was discussed, but after I submitted my estimate as to how long this would take from where we were, the subject was not mentioned again.

Expecting to meet up again at the next town we each departed separately, but it was the last I saw of either of them. That night I slept for the first time on grass by a lovely clear river with enough water in it to completely submerge oneself.

During the course of the drive on the following day I was

stopped and escorted by jeep through the military zone, a stretch of about thirty-five miles.

During the course of the three-day drive to Ankara I went through the towns of Erzurum, Erzincan, Sivas and Kayseri; the country in parts became mountainous, with good scenery. My first encounter with rain occurred on the way to Kayseri, causing high jinks on the muddy road surface.

Ankara for me meant that I had successfully made the trip home and the rest was just a formality. I had been told by a couple travelling the other way that from Ankara to England one followed a tarmac road all the way. Having decided to spend a couple of days in Istanbul instead of Ankara I was soon using the power so long stifled in the bike. Whilst in Istanbul I went into a shop to change a rather large note into something small to pay a rascal of a hotel-keeper who was trying to cheat me. When the owner of the shop arrived he began to tell how he had lived in London and for several years in Leeds, where he had attended the university. He took me in hand, and fixed me up in his uncle's hotel, then took me out to dine in a very smart restaurant where I had the best meal I'd eaten for over six months. As I was staying in a fairly rough quarter of the city, a café proprietor insisted that I leave the bike in the restaurant which enabled me to sleep easier, although it meant rising at six in time to pull it out before opening time.

After locating the consulate and obtaining the Yugoslav visa I left Istanbul and headed for Bulgaria wondering what an Iron Curtain country would be like. I arrived at the border in the early morning and was refused entry on account of having no visa. I had been misinformed at the Consulate, and had to return to the border town of Edirne and obtain one from the Consulate there.

On entering Bulgaria I noticed at once how neat and orderly everything was, tree-lined roads with all the stones along the roadside painted white, all dead leaves swept into piles, an absence of advertisements. In fact it was like an army camp. People with whom I had contact were very polite and efficient, they almost seemed afraid to be anything else. Driving along these roads was in fact quite pleasant, mostly farming country on each side. One of the large towns, Plovdiv, seemed very plain; I can barely remember it at all. Unfortunately before I arrived at my hoped-for destination, Sofia, I had a back-wheel puncture: a nail which I had noticed embedded in the tyre in Iran eventually burst it. With the help of a passing motorcyclist I was soon on my way to Sofia. This town I liked very much, clean with several very nice buildings, one in particular with a gold-coloured roof. An obvious foreigner walking around with a camera seems to give every policeman the idea that he's just found himself a spy. After several hours wandering and a meal I drove off to the Yugoslav frontier some thirty miles away.

This frontier crossing proved to be the stormiest of the whole trip. A huge fat Italian, obviously very wealthy, had all his money spread on the table, Canadian dollars, American dollars, and several heaps of other currency, all being meticulously counted by the officer. Unable to understand a word of what was being said, I guessed that there was a great danger of him losing the money, as he seemed to blubber any second. Standing by the gate the customs officers gave me back my *carnet* and passport, then asked if I had any money. Thinking he intended to change my money, as did the fellow on my entry, I handed him about £3 10s. in leva. When no money came forth I asked him about it. All he said was 'Confiscate' and as far as I could see, to him that was the end of the business. Roused to fighting fury by this cool cheek, I started a riot which finished with the guard running from the gate with fixed bayonet, and myself cursing the officer and telling him if he touched me with it, I'd shove it up his waistcoat. Quite surprised that anyone should dare say anything at all in this country, he wrote out an official form to me to draw the money from the *Banc de Bulgarie* in Erchard. Sure that no such bank existed, I drove into Yugoslavia still seething with rage. Ten minutes later a passing car flung a stone straight through my headlamp.

My first experience of a town in Yugoslavia put me on my guard against policemen. I was fined 10 shillings on the spot for a miserable parking offence. Determined that 'Big Brother' should get no more money for his next rocket from me, I drove very warily. The ride to Belgrade, some of the way on the 'Autoput', was quite pleasant, though not of any particular interest. Along the 'Autoput' which connects Belgrade and Zagreb, I was travelling fairly slowly, looking for a good spot to sleep the night. I was surprised by a man in uniform waving me down. Thinking quickly, I knew that I was breaking no laws, so I stopped, with the engine ticking over. It was a policeman. 'You are travelling too fast, comrade,' he said in bad English. I shook my head and said 'Autoput'. He then made a sign which I knew at once: money. Shoving the bike into gear, I let out the clutch and drove off with him grabbing at my shoulders. With a good hefty hand-off I was rid of him, and motored down the road for a couple of hours at a steady 75mph.

A second 'Autoput' from Zagreb goes to Ljubljana and here the countryside takes an almost Swiss look, small chalets and churches on the mountainside. Within a short time after leaving Ljubljana I arrived at the Italian border, expecting both trouble from the customs and sunshine. I got neither. Almost casually I passed through the formalities, to be greeted by torrential rain which continued almost all the way from Trieste to Manchester. From Trieste I followed the 'Autostrada' through Milan and Turin, with a gripping ride over a snowbound pass from Turin into France. A pleasant evening was spent in a pub-cum-café playing the locals at a football game, in the ski resort of Modane. Then a bee-line for Boulogne. Three days later, after terrible weather and damp nights in hayricks, I landed at Dover after a rough Channel crossing to be greeted by the report: 'Floods all over the country'.

A night in a transport café, a puncture on the M1, and at midnight in teeming rain I stood outside the house I had left six months ago. A few pebbles at the bedroom window soon had Audrey, my wife, down to greet me with a pint of tea and a big fire. The date was Friday, 4 November 1960.

TED SIMON

JUPITER'S TRAVELS

Ted Simon was brought up in London the son of a German mother and Romanian father. He gave up a potential career as a scientist in favour of journalism and worked for a number of newspapers and magazines.

In 1973 at the age of 42 he decided to submit to his wanderlust and embarked upon a phenomenal 78,000-mile journey around the world on a 500cc Triumph Tiger motorcycle. The story of this epic, *Jupiter's Travels* (1979), became a bestseller and is regarded as a classic of the genre. Remarkably, in 2001 aged 69 he decided to repeat the journey related in his book, *Dreaming of Jupiter* (2007), which *Motorcycle News* referred to as 'the greatest motorcycle travel book – part two!'

Ted Simon lives in Northern California.

So sure had I been that I would not get through that I had not once considered where I would head for if I did. I had not even thought about petrol. Holding my map under the headlight I saw that there was a pump at Sidi Barani, fifty miles along. I seemed to arrive there in no time at all. There was fuel, but nowhere to stay. The town, if there was one, had melted into darkness.

Eighty five miles to Mersa Matruh. Nothing. I felt like riding all night, to Cairo if necessary.

Ten miles short of Matruh I saw some painted oil barrels across the road, with a hurricane lamp burning on one of them. Light shone from the doorway of a little hut. I slowed down and a soldier approached me. He laid his left arm across his right wrist and opened his right hand, palm upwards, in the sign that meant 'Papers!'

I stopped, unlocked the box and brought out the passport. An older man in pyjamas and fez came out of the hut.

'Please wait,' he said. 'It will be ten minutes only.'

I heard a manual telephone cranking and lit a cigarette. After a while a third man came out and got into a black car parked beyond the barrier. As he started the engine and drove off the man in pyjamas hurried over to me.

'Follow that car, please,' he said urgently. 'They will clear you in Matruh if you hurry, but they are just going to close down.'

I was infected by the slight sense of panic and rushed off. The car was doing over seventy miles an hour and I had some difficulty catching it. Then, for the second time that day, the bowels of the earth slid open beneath me. I reached back with my right hand. The lid of the box had been blown off. Expecting to put the passport back, I had not locked it again. I stopped immediately. The wallet had gone. I looked at the mileage indicator. It could have happened anywhere in the last six miles.

The wallet contained driving licences, vaccination certificates, credit cards, photographs, currency and an address book. Losing it seemed like an overwhelming disaster. Two cholera shots, a yellow-fever shot and a smallpox vaccination would have to be done again. There were addresses I might never recover. The cash, the credit cards were extra layers of defence stripped away. But how far could I get without a driving licence?

Slowly I drove back, on the wrong side of the road, searching but numbed by this sudden reverse in my fortunes. I had ridden nearly four hundred miles that day, and the weariness hit me then. I tried to think clearly. The gloves should have been the last objects to fall, and as they were quite bulky I hoped to see them where a black wallet might not show.

For a mile I saw nothing. Then I saw light ahead, and the murmur of engines running. I came across two taxis, one coming, one going, stopped alongside each other with their interior lights on. One driver was in the middle of the road, a tall bearded man in white robe and turban. He stood in the space carved out of the darkness by the car lights, and seemed very much in command of that space. I wanted to stop and ask whether he had seen anything, but he waved me on peremptorily. His hand was raised in a threatening way and he stared at me fiercely. I felt too weak to resist, and rode on.

I went on searching vainly until I got back to the police post. A truck was coming through, and the police commandeered it to help me search in the much brighter illumination of its headlights. After a while I found the lid of the box. Then the truck driver spotted the first glove, and soon after I saw the second one. The wallet should have been between the lid and the gloves. I went up and down several times but found nothing.

I was in a state of despair out of all proportion to the disaster. Weariness, the end of a long day, me alone with the bike at midnight in a strange country at war; that was part of it. From Mark Antony to Charlie Brown in one thoughtless moment. I snatched at the lesson. As always I felt I could endure my tribulations if there was something to be learned from them. *Euphoria leads to thoughtlessness.* That's how fortunes are told. So OK. No more mindless chasing after cars. *Is that all?*

No, that was not all. I went over the incident again in my mind, saw the Arab standing in that pool of light in the darkness, with his arm raised. Yes, but I had seen something else, before I had even known what I was looking at. I had seen him straightening up, that was it, straightening his legs. He had been rising from the road surface and I had seen him do it but I had not wanted to know because I was too tired. No! Not too tired, too *frightened*. I was too frightened of that imperious wave of the hand, of that fierce glance, to face up to the fact that he had just found my wallet on the road.

The discovery was devastating. I had thought I was a man. I had taken risks and come through them in the way a man was supposed to, and yet here I was after all just a boy quailing before the first figure of authority that came my way. It went very deep in me, this fear of authority, and it sickened me to find myself as vulnerable as ever. I knew the robed figure would haunt me for a long time. It was the beginning of a long struggle.

Hard as it was to bear this moment of self-realization, I found some kind of strength in it. I piled up some stones to mark the place where I had been searching and rode on to the checkpoint at Matruh where I was given back my passport. I explained what I was doing, and went back on with the search, but with no more success than before.

Then I started thinking. If the Arab had taken the wallet, he would probably not keep it. He would take what was valuable and throw away the rest. Where? Before the checkpoint. I rode up to the first checkpoint again, and worked back. The driver of a car going to Libya would throw something from his window across the road to the other side. But no. In Libya traffic drives on the right, in Egypt on the left. So it would be a left-hand drive car, driving on the left of the road. I followed the right-hand verge going towards Matruh. Fifty yards along I saw a small bundle of paper against the root of a bush. The wallet had been broken in half. No money. No address section. No photographs. No credit cards. But the vaccination certificates were there, and one international driving licence. I could find nothing more in the area. Partly relieved, and a little better pleased with myself, I returned to Matruh.

Having arrived in Alexandria:
I carried out my first-ever major motorcycle overhaul in Alexandria. Both pistons, I found, were deformed by heat, and I had only one spare piston with me (a piece of nonsense which inspired more waves of telepathic profanity to burn the ears of Meriden). I found a cavernous garage near Ramilies Station and haggled bitterly over five piastres for the right to work there,

and then received many times that amount back in tea, cigarettes, snacks, and true friendship from the poor men who struggled to earn a livelihood in that place.

I took two days to do a job that might have been done in two or three hours, but every move was fraught with danger. Already I knew that there would be no chance at all of getting spare parts in Egypt. I dared not make a mistake. The pistons had seized their rings, and I replaced the less distorted one after sculpting the slots with a razor blade. It seemed the only thing to do. I prayed that I was right. I had no real idea about what had caused the overheating after only four thousand miles, and felt rather gloomy about it.

There were many British motorcycles pumping round the streets and some shops still had stocks of parts for them, but they were single-cylinder BSAs, Enfields, AJSs of ancient vintage. It was warming to see all these old British bikes plodding on after twenty years or more, and obviously held in high esteem, but it was rather pathetic also. I knew that it was only economic policy that prevented them importing new machines, and that small Japanese bikes would be much better suited to them. If the Japanese ever got a foothold, British bikes would quickly become only a nostalgic memory. There was so much goodwill towards us that it seemed criminal to fritter it away, yet we had nothing to offer now in competition.

When the Triumph was all buttoned up again I tested it rather nervously. The first clouds of smoke frightened the life out of me but when the excess oil was burned away, it ran clean and sounded fine.

JONATHAN GREGSON

Extract from

BULLET UP THE GRAND TRUNK ROAD

Jonathan Gregson was born in Calcutta in India. Having started off his writing career as a city journalist on the *Sunday Telegraph* he became a travel and business writer and has contributed articles for publications such as *Time Out, Condé Nast Traveler, National Geographic,* the *Financial Times, Fortune* and the *Wall Street Journal* amongst others.

He has written three books, including *Bullet up the Grand Trunk Road* (1997) which tells of a 1,600-mile motorcycle journey on an Indian-manufactured Royal Enfield Bullet from Calcutta to the North-West Frontier and uses the mirror of the conflagration of Partition in 1947 as a study of the modern-day sub-continent.

We crossed the new road bridge over the Indus and drew up on the far bank. Looking back, the rounded bastions of Attock Fort glowed in the afternoon sun. Further downstream was the village from which boatmen had once ferried travellers across the monsoon-swollen river, while in the dry season a boat-bridge was strung together.

Sarah was just reaching for her camera when a shout rang out.

A policeman was running towards us, wagging his finger in disapproval. 'No pictures,' he yelled. 'Attock Fort, Army Property, no pictures. Road bridge, also no pictures.'

I'd met this kind of official paranoia in India, but up to now not in Pakistan. For a nasty moment I thought he was going to try and confiscate the camera. But once the offending object had been put back in its case, the policeman was all smiles and waved us through the border check-point.

To begin with the road curled beside the Landai River, which carries the combined waters of the Kabul and Swat rivers down to their junction with the Indus. Then the surrounding hills opened up and we entered the Vale of Peshawar, a land beloved of the Mughals, its rolling valleys and sparkling streams being excelled in their estimation only by that other valley surrounded by mountains, the Vale of Kashmir.

As we had been travelling north along the Grand Trunk

Road we had kept up with the change of seasons, and here in the borderlands it was first spring once more. The raised edges of fields glittered with wild flowers; the willow and the plane trees were just coming into bud; and there was a sharpness in the air carried down from the snow-capped Hindu Kush. A road sign announced that there were only forty miles to Peshawar. I was looking forward to celebrating the end of our journey in style under the ramparts of the Bala Hisar.

The Grand Trunk Road again broadened out into a four-lane highway and we were going flat out just to keep pace with the local taxis and mini-buses – the Pathans seemingly even more addicted to speed than their Punjabi brethren. Then, beyond the garrison town of Nowshera, we ran into a series of road-works.

Even on this unmade surface the faster traffic, private cars and pick-ups converted into taxis, kept overtaking and cutting in at the last minute. I was trying to keep up with the pace, jockeying for position, when the road-works suddenly stopped and we bumped through a succession of muddy potholes and back onto a metalled surface.

I accelerated to get clear of the pack but there was no traction whatsoever between the rear tyre and the road. Instead of speeding up, the bike started to roll from side to side. I struggled to correct the steering, but the back end was swinging around, completely out of control. The next thing I knew the bike was on its side and my head was skidding along the tarmac. Somehow my helmet had got wedged between the handlebars and the road surface.

We were splayed out across the middle of the Grand Trunk

Road. All I could think about was the line of trucks coming up behind us, ready to crush us beneath their huge tyres.

'Get out of here,' I shouted to Sarah, but her leg was trapped beneath the weight of the bike. She was yelling at me, something about a bus coming. With my head pinned to the tarmac I couldn't see much. But she could look backwards and what she saw was a bus bearing down on us.

We were saved by the driver of a private car who deliberately swerved, placing his vehicle in between us and the heavy traffic. The bus's tyres came into my line of vision. I felt the vibration in my bones, waited for the sickening crunch. Nothing came. The bus driver must have swerved to avoid the car, and in doing so he also steered clear of the fallen bike.

We crawled out from underneath the Bullet and ran for the safety of the roadside. The heavy trucks rumbled past without hitting us. The car driver reversed his vehicle immediately behind the overturned bike, providing a barrier against the onrush of traffic. He then helped me pick up the Enfield and wheel it over to the side of the road.

I was trying to thank him for having saved our lives – incoherently, forgetting even to ask his name. 'It is nothing,' he said. 'Please now check if you are injured.'

Sarah was clutching her left elbow, the side we'd come down on. By some miracle her felt jacket hadn't split open, but underneath it she had gravel burns and bruising.

It was only when I removed my own helmet that I realised how lucky I'd been. The chin guard was deeply scoured. If I hadn't been wearing a full-face helmet I'd have lost half my jaw. I reached for a cigarette when the man who'd stopped his car to help us shouted something. Petrol. The bloody stuff had leaked out over the road.

I put back my lighter and examined the fuel tank. Strange, nothing seemed to be leaking. Then the car driver pointed down the road. 'Benzine,' he shouted.

The whole surface was covered with an amalgam of mud and diesel fuel. A tanker or lorry must have spilled some of its load coming through the bumpy section before rejoining the asphalt road, which would explain why it had felt like a skating rink when I opened up the throttle.

I reassured the driver that neither of us needed to be taken to hospital. 'Very good,' he said. 'But will your machine also be working?'

I looked over the Bullet. The headlight had been smashed, the handlebars were scoured, an indicator was missing. But apart from that there were no obvious signs of damage. I supposed that while I was waltzing down the road we must have lost most of our forward momentum, so that by the time the bike went on its side we'd been travelling quite slowly. I tried the ignition switch and it worked. I walked wearily around to the kick-start. The engine didn't fire on the first try, but the system obviously still functioned.

Sarah was leaning up against a tree, dragging on a cigarette. I joined her and asked if she felt up to getting back on the bike. 'Right now it's the last thing I want to do in this world. But, OK, I suppose we've only got another twenty miles to go.'

Half an hour later we limped into Peshawar. The steering felt wobbly as hell and, to tell the truth, so did I. We didn't bother to stop under the ramparts of Bala Hisar Fort; it wasn't exactly the joyous entry I had envisaged.

We'd made it to the end of the Grand Trunk Road – on the map 1,600 miles from where we'd started out in Calcutta, though in fact the mileometer showed that we'd covered almost twice that distance. But the accident down the road had robbed us of any sense of achievement. I felt numb as I pulled into the driveway of Dean's Hotel and cut the engine. A marquee was being erected for a wedding feast or some other celebration. Sarah pulled herself wearily out of the saddle. 'Just thank God,' she said, 'we're still alive.'

JONNY BEALBY

Extract from

RUNNING WITH THE MOON

Jonny Bealby was born in 1963 and was educated in England, Scotland and Canada. He has had a wide variety of jobs including stunt horse rider, singer in a band and motorcycle courier. Whilst travelling in Kashmir his fiancée Melanie was suddenly taken ill and tragically died. Two years later, still devastated by the loss of her, he embarked upon a daring, highly dangerous and emotionally charged journey across Africa on a Yamaha Ténéré related in his book *Running with The Moon* (1995). Highly acclaimed by the critics for this endearing, moving and courageous tale, he went on to write *For a Pagan Song* (1998) and *Silk Dreams, Troubled Road* (2003).

He now runs the adventure travel company Wild Frontiers.

It was six fifteen in the morning and I saw with tired resentment that the rear wheel of the bike was flat again, not totally, but about two-thirds of the way down. It was no way to start the day, especially when I had hopes of driving the full 370 miles to the border. I debated just pumping the tyre up and hoping for the best but thought better of it. I got the wheel off, took out the damaged inner tube and put the new one in, but being too hasty as usual I caught it with the tyre lever and tore an inch-long gash in it just below the valve. Cursing to myself I took it out again, got my patches from the box and stuck one over the hole. This time, taking a good deal more care, I put it back in and pumped it up. Oily and sweaty I set off, crossing my fingers that I had been served my quota of trouble for the day. But only a few miles out of town that familiar sensation of riding on jelly hit me again. Another blow-out. I discovered that I had actually put the patch on the wrong way up.

As I sat on the ground changing the patch an army truck approached from the direction of the town. It stopped just in front of the bike and ten or so red-bereted UNITA soldiers alighted and gathered round. I was too pissed off to be afraid; besides, they were all smiling and, as far as any African soldier can, they looked benign.

Their Captain was a very large man with a round flat face

as black as his combat boots. The soldiers' camouflage uniforms were clean and pressed, their backs were straight and, as Jack had said, they appeared to be well-disciplined and professional. I got it across that I was going to the border via Lubango and they offered to escort me some of the way, telling me in mime and Portuguese that I had inadvertently taken a wrong turning in town and was actually heading back to Lobito. The second puncture fixed, more oily and sweaty than ever, I set off behind my personal armed escort feeling fairly confident that those arms would not be turned on me.

The road started to climb from sea level back onto the sandstone plateau. My good Samaritans moved slowly before me and at last I managed to enjoy the day. A few more miles down the road and the wheel blew again. My cup of misery was full.

'FUUUCK!' I swore as I slithered to the side of the road. Three punctures in ten miles was too much to bear, but bear it I had to for short of putting the bike on the soldiers' truck, there was nothing else to do.

To my relief the soldiers stopped and came back, all sympathy. It was a dangerous place to be stuck, at the mercy of any passerby, and I was thankful for their protection. The rip in the inner tube had now reached the valve and was beyond repair, leaving me no option but to replace it with the one I'd found semi-deflated earlier that morning.

Forty minutes later we were under way again. Then the drive chain started to slip, missing every few turns on the front sprocket and so losing me power. Was this going to be a stage of the journey blighted by ghosts in the machinery? Not yet, I prayed, at least hold together to see me into safer territory.

The dark mountains, jutting almost vertically out of the earth, became larger the further east we travelled. Nestling in their lee, there were more homesteads, mud and wooden *kraals* set back off the road, though it was hard to see what was actually farmed. At Caraculo the soldiers explained they could go no further. They all shook my hand ceremoniously and wished me luck, with the Captain advising me to stay at Lubango, on top of the escarpment, rather than risk driving at night to the border; this time I vowed to take the advice. It was impossible for me to believe that any of these men could be connected with murder. They had gone about 150 miles out of their way to see me safely through their area. I only wished I could keep them with me to the frontier.

Since Namibe the road had been flat and straight; it now began its serpentine climb into the clouds, coiling powerfully one way then the other through looping hairpin bends. Two large trucks crawled painfully up the steep incline in bottom gear, swinging out wide, using what limited space there was to see their long back-ends safely round the corners. Here the chain slip became more of a problem. As I arched round each of the bends the front cog slipped through the chain leaving momentum my only form of propulsion. On the straight stretches its bite was better and I was able to push past the trucks. To my surprise they were driven by whites.

The mountainside was thick with vegetation. Exquisite red flowers on long, elegant stems, orchids perhaps, nodded their heads in the breeze as I passed. Up and up I went, ever closer to the distant mist. A few hundred feet before the top, just below the clouds, the road levelled out and ran along a ledge. Looking back, the view was unbroken, holding no buildings, no people. A place that was as old as the earth itself.

Soon after one o'clock I came over a ridge and found Lubango nestling in a valley below me, guarded by an effigy of the Madonna, high on the opposite hill. After some difficulty I found a place to stay and store my bike. When I looked at the chain to check its strength I realised that the slippage was because I hadn't replaced the wheel correctly after the last puncture. I fixed it before going to rest in the hotel.

Sitting on my musty bed going through my wallet I realized that, after all, I did not have enough local currency to see me out of Angola. I had of course been keeping an eye on the situation as I knew it would be close, but, in short, I'd got it wrong. I had enough to pay for the hotel and to buy some supper but even if I went without that, I would still be a couple of thousand kwanzas short of what I needed for petrol. This was a problem as I only had one fifty-pound travellers' cheque left. I was fairly confident that I would be able to cash it, but not so confident that I would be able to change into rand the sixty or seventy thousand kwanzas I would have left when I reached Namibia. This would leave me in a new country without so much as a bent penny until I could find a bank to give me some cash on my Mastercard.

The first couple of banks would not accept travellers' cheques but at the third, the Bank of Agriculture, I had more luck. It being a Friday, the bank was packed inside and out and I had some trouble getting in at all. The guard insisted that the bank was now closed but after I'd pleaded and begged, and taken the gamble of slipping him a 1,000-kwanza note, he finally allowed me entry. Inside, the noise and smoke from a thousand cigarettes made it feel more like a pub at last orders than a bank. I was taken round the back, away from the throng of punters clamouring at the tills, to a quiet small office. An attractive lady appeared and informed me that the official rate was 1,000 to the pound and gave me, after bank charges, over 70,000 kwanzas. I couldn't imagine how I would spend even half of it. A reasonable dinner would be a start . . .

The road south from Lubango to the border had been almost destroyed by the sixteen years of fighting. What was marked on my map as a smooth-surfaced road had been turned by bombs, landmines and strafing jets into a battleground of rubble and craters. At times even the suggestion of an asphalt surface was gone. A thick layer of mud, pocked with deep pot-holes, was all that remained of the only route south. It was agonizingly slow work weaving around the craters, like trying to stay on the ridges of a honeycomb. At times I missed the line completely, plunging myself into ankle-deep water, and once I was thrown off-balance by a particularly large hole and forced off the road down a steep bank to a boggy marsh below. I held my breath while I scrambled the bike back up to the track.

'Oh ja, there's still plenty of active mines out there,' Rolf, one of the Afrikaner truck drivers I'd seen coming from Namibe, had happily informed me in a restaurant the previous evening, 'so be sure to stick to the tracks. Only three days ago I saw a cow get it. Blew the fuckin' thing sky high.' He had laughed maniacally at the memory and slapped his hand on the frail table. He told me the drivers had christened it Desolation Road.

'What about bandits,' I'd asked, 'are there any?'

'Jesus man, are you green? Of course there are fuckin' bandits. Why do you think they pay me 25,000 rand a trip?' While he'd downed half the contents of his can in one gulp I worked it out. Five thousand pounds for a ten-day journey. I could barely believe it. ''Struth man, these guys would fuckin' kill you for a packet of Marlboro. I'm telling you for nothing, get your bloody head down and go for it . . . Ugh . . . it's no place for sightseeing.'

And that's exactly what I did, but it was far from easy. Rain had been coming down most of the night and started again soon after I had left the town. At Chibia I tried to fill up with petrol as there had been another of the frequent power cuts in Lubango. Unfortunately the same was true here so the pumps didn't work. The lanky attendant told me he had fifteen litres stashed away which I could have at a black market price. As money was one thing I was not short of I accepted but I doubted it would be enough fuel to see me through to Namibia.

For thirty miles the road improved and I managed to make up some time. On top of the plateau dense stretches of thorn and acacia, grass and baobabs sprouted prosperously from the deep red earth. I passed Rolf's empty truck, its cargo of Castle beer safely deposited in the bars of Namibe. Two more such journeys and he would have the money to buy the ranch he wanted up here.

'I don't want no fuckin' Communist ruling me,' he had said in reference to the ANC. 'I'll buy my land, fence in the cattle and get the fuckin' kaffirs to work for shit.' If that was all Angola had to look forward to after the elections I wondered how long it would be till the next war.

For the next fifty miles the roads could not have been in worse condition. The way was brown with mud, not grey with tar, slippery and wet. Some of the craters were so large you could lose a car in them, and all were full of muddy water. Up and down I'd go through the filth, stopping every few miles to pump up my ever-deflating tyre, all the while paranoid that I might meet bandits. I would have tried driving through the bush at the bottom of the road's grassy bank had it not been for the warning about unexploded mines. There was nothing to do but battle on. Not knowing how long it would last I kept looking hopefully into the distance for clear grey patches of asphalt. Sometimes they materialised but they were always short-lived and soon returned me to the gauntlet of Desolation Road.

At least the rain had stopped, allowing the sun to beat its way through the retreating clouds. Every so often, near a village, I'd pass some cattle and a herdsman walking next to the road. 'Go home,' I'd think. But the cattle had to be grazed and the herdsman had to be with them. Mines or no mines.

Most of the once-picturesque villages were now bombed-out shells, some completely deserted. Walls, painted with murals of Castro and Lenin, were smashed, the heavy concrete and twisted girders looking as though they'd been dumped there by trucks and had never formed homes. At Xangongo the bridge over the Cunene river had been destroyed in an air-raid. All that remained, trailing pathetically in the brown torrent, was tangled metal and shattered stone. A makeshift pontoon bridge had been placed further along and I trundled over it and up the other side, where I found a tumbledown bar. Spent shell cases served as flower pots outside and inside was dark and dusty. It belonged to a middle-aged woman with a mild manner who said I would find no petrol in this town, but maybe in Ondjiva a further fifty kilometres on. Throughout the war she had kept the bar open, she told me, catering for the Cubans and now for UN officials and the truck drivers.

South of Xangongo the road, a thin corridor through the now receding bush, improved enormously. This was surprising as the signs of war were more evident than ever. Burnt-out tanks, trucks, armoured personnel carriers, fuel bowsers, even helicopters lay rusting where they had died or been pushed to clear the road. The jagged metal and torn shapes took on hideous forms – ugly beasts from an evil world left to rot in the scorching heat.

I almost laughed when I reached Ondjiva, an hour or so later. This was where I wanted to stay the night? There was barely a building left standing and those few that were were so badly scarred by bullets and crippled by mortars or bombs as to be practically useless. Countless civilians must have died in this destroyed town. It was a damning indictment of the South Africans and exposed their lie that 'our boys' only hit military targets. In a ruined church a young female teacher defied the conditions and led her class through a lesson. The children sat on the rubble under the open sky. What future, I wondered, did they have?

In the street nothing moved save the wind and the dust. Thin, war-weary faces looked out of glassless windows. Girders creaked. There was no hotel, no petrol, and no food. A ghost town full of ghosts. How long would it take to get that community back to some semblance of normality? One thing was for sure, whoever did get power in the elections would have a mighty job on their hands. There was nothing for me to do but carry on to the border in the vain hope that my petrol supply would last the thirty miles.

The track now was white with chalky stones and still potholed. The verdure had disappeared once more, leaving dry sparse bush. I turned on the reserve petrol as I left the town and drove as steadily as possible in an attempt to conserve what fuel I had. It was not enough though and about five miles before the frontier the engine cut out. Still high, the sun was beating down from a clear sky and the slight breeze brought little relief. But there was no alternative, I had to push.

After a few minutes, with sweat already dripping off my face, I heard a vehicle approaching from behind. I stopped, welcoming the rest, and turned to see a white Range Rover pulling up alongside.

'Howzit, you got a problem?' I could tell by the trapped nasal accent that he was an Afrikaner. He was about fifty and was travelling with a boy, who might have been his son, and an old, smiling African with greying hair.

'You could say that,' I panted, 'I need some petrol to get me to the border.'

'Well then, it's your lucky day,' he said, getting out of the car. 'You don't want to hang around here you know, it might not be so good for your health.' He smiled and took a twenty-litre jerry can from the boot, along with a large plastic funnel, and made towards the bike.

'I should warn you, I don't have any rand or dollars, only kwanzas.'

'Ah, don't sweat it, I can spare a few litres.'

I undid the petrol tank and he started to pour.

'You'll need enough to get to Ondangwa,' he said reflectively, 'you'll not find any at the border. It's quite a machine you got there. How many ks does she do?'

'Oh . . . quite a few, six or seven to the litre. A gallon should be enough.' I was very thankful for this show of generosity and I couldn't help wondering if I might be able to push it a little further. 'I don't suppose you would swap my kwanzas for a few rand would you? Make it worth your while . . . I mean, anything would be good. They're useless to me and, like I say, I've no hard cash.'

'I'm afraid they'd be just about as useless to me, too,' he said, returning to the rear of his car. 'I don't think I'll be back up here for a while, but I'll see.' He threw the can into the boot and climbed back in. 'We'll see you at the border, maybe I can help you there. It's no good hanging around out here.' With a short wave and a smile he moved the long gearstick into first and left in a cloud of dust.

Such was the state of the road it took me twenty minutes to reach the customs post where I found the white car parked outside the immigration office. After the formalities were completed the kindly Afrikaner handed me fifty rand, about a tenner, for the 50,000 kwanzas I had left. Even though the rate of exchange was diabolical I was extremely grateful.

'How are the roads from here?' I asked wearily, once the transaction was complete. 'I hope they're better than these'

They looked at me with mocking astonishment, the father placing a hand on my shoulder. 'Are you joking? . . . the roads? . . . better? I don't know how long you've been stuck up there in the bush fella, but you're about to rejoin civilisation. And, if you don't mind me saying so,' he turned to the others, 'you look as though you could use some!'

While they laughed I pondered the word. *Civilisation . . . yes.* I tossed it around in my head for a moment, lingering on each syllable: what a wonderful sound it had. It would mean a road, straight and flat, without pot-holes. It would mean shops with provisions that I actually wanted and food that was pleasant to eat. It would mean hotels with electricity, showers with hot water and bedrooms without insects or rats. It would mean people not wearied by war and aggression, and it meant the Cape and the completion of my original journey. In short, it meant everything.

'There's a hotel in town called the Three A's,' the father was saying, 'you can't miss it. It's cheap and clean. Do yourself a favour and stay the night.' Smiling they wished me luck and drifted back to their car.

An hour later as I studied my reflection in the hotel mirror I realised that his remarks had been justified. I looked a mess. I hadn't shaved since Soyo, the venue of my last proper wash. My skin was both stained with dirt and burnt by the sun. My lips were cracked and my hair lank. Little more than oily rags were left of my jeans and my T-shirt had fared no better. However, when I looked into my eyes I saw a sparkle I had not seen for many a day. They seemed bluer – as though a cloud had been lifted – full of energy and life. Even if it was still a little bruised, my body beneath the rags was lean and fit. Not only had I almost achieved my initial goal, but I knew I'd actually enjoyed doing it. All that aggro: the endurance across the desert, the seemingly endless fight through the jungle and the constant fear of attack in the land I'd just passed through were what I had wanted. I had left England for adventure and I had found it.

My hotel room had an electric fan and clean cotton sheets. The shower was hot and the taste of the succulent fillet steak indescribable. I sat on the veranda afterwards, *real* scotch whisky in hand, looking up at the moon, and tried to take it all in. I had put myself in the hands of something bigger and had been rewarded. Wherever I decided to go, whichever route I took, I now felt I'd make it. It seemed I had been chosen.

Holding the drink up to my far-off friend I swirled it round, enjoying the moment of anticipation as the ice clinked gently against the glass. I took a long pull and let the smooth, fiery liquid rest on my tongue, the flavour filling my mouth as it reached each taste-bud in turn. I held it there for an age, reluctant to let it go. Then, with a final swish through my teeth, I let it slip down my throat. It tingled sweetly all the way down. 'Yes,' I thought, 'civilisation . . . hello there.'

LOIS PRYCE

Extract from

LOIS ON THE LOOSE

Having left school at 16, Lois Pryce worked amongst other things as a carrot picker, painter and decorator and record shop assistant before trusting her instincts, grabbing her Yamaha XT225 Serow and embarking on an extraordinary 20,000-mile journey from the most northerly tip of Alaska to Ushuaia, Tierra del Fuego at the limits of the continent of South America. Funny, ballsy and unfailingly passionate, *Lois on the Loose* (2007) is highly entertaining and shows Lois to be full of the spirit that inspired such amazing female pioneers of motorcycle travel as Theresa Wallach.

Not content with conquering the Americas, Lois followed this by crossing Africa, an epic journey related in *Red Tape and White Knuckles* (2008).

I wondered what all the fuss was about as I glided through the Guatemala entry formalities. These Central American border crossings had a terrible reputation for bribe-hungry policemen, corrupt officials and hours of soul-destroying bureaucracy, but here I was in the customs office being processed in the most able fashion by an efficient, incorruptible young woman and surrounded by Government notices encouraging their people to say NO! to bribery. Other than an entrepreneurial man hovering outside with a pressure washer, who half-heartedly sprayed the wheels of my bike in an unsuccessful attempt to charge me for 'fumigación' services, I was pretty much left alone to wade undisturbed through the mayhem of Mesilla.

Never before had I encountered such a concentrated number of humans per square foot; even the road itself was so jam-packed with bodies that I had to slow down to crawling pace until I was forced to put my feet on the road and paddle my way through the throng. The border town reminded me of a mini-Tijuana without the tourists, bustling with the air of an ancient trading post where folk from each neighbouring country would come to barter and haggle over one another's wares.

But my romantic image of exotic spices and hand-tooled leather saddles changing hands for gold bars or silver handled pistols was dashed by the reality of knock-off Nike trainers and mountains of cheap Tupperware.

Despite the abundance of bogus designer sportswear, it was an exciting entry into this new stage of my journey. As the crowd thinned out and the frenetic hustle of the town ebbed away, I followed the Pan American Highway through a lush, verdant river valley that glowed luminous green with giant ferns and exotic plants boasting leaves big enough to sleep under. The skyline was dominated by a range of black volcanoes, jutting into the heavens like a Jonathan Aitken polygraph reading, their peaks obscured by the clouds that hovered patiently all day, waiting to deliver the rainy season's regular daily deluge.

All along the road, the people of Guatemala were going about their business, the women dressed in their traditional brightly patterned shawls and long skirts, while the men opted for a more sombre look in dark Western-style clothes. Children and old folk alike carried colossal bundles of firewood on their backs, women effortlessly bore baskets of fruit on their heads and the men tended the goats and sheep. I felt as though I'd been transported back to a bygone age, and for the first time since leaving England, I was acutely aware of being in a distant, faraway land. Even in Mexico, enough dribs and drabs of Western civilization had seeped over the border from the USA to remind me it was still out there, and the long stretches of mountain scenery and pine trees had provided me with no big surprises. But here in this corner of Guatemala, there were absolutely no visible references to life as I knew it. Heading for the old colonial city of Antigua, the fairytale feel intensified as the road began to climb steeply towards the volcanoes until I reached such an altitude that I was riding through the very clouds I had been gazing at earlier.

I'd always had this image of the Pan American Highway as a grand slice of multi-lane, international motorway traversing half the globe, but I was quickly getting used to the idea that it was little more than a title given to a collection of major routes that linked up across the continent, and that what passed for a major route in the USA or Canada was very different from here in the Banana Republics, with their legacies of civil war, earthquakes and scatterings of landmines to add to the fun. In Mexico, the highway was known as the Inter-Americana, here it was the CA–1 – *Centro Americana Uno* – but whatever its name, it was often no more than a narrow rural road, and this leg was as rough going as a farm track, littered with gaping potholes, and long stretches where Mother Nature had successfully beaten back her arch-enemy, the mighty blacktop.

I studied the map, examining my course through this isthmus of tiny Central American countries: Guatemala, El Salvador, Honduras, Nicaragua, Costa Rica, Panama. Some of them were so small, I'd be crossing a border every day or so. With the exception of Costa Rica maybe, none of them jumped out at me as a popular holiday destination. I recalled some of the more memorable snippets from the Foreign Office travel advice website:

Travellers in smaller vehicles have been targeted by armed robbers after crossing the Honduran border. Hmm, smaller vehicles? Well, I guess a motorcycle would fall into that category.

Dengue fever and malaria are endemic to Nicaragua, outbreaks tend to increase in the rainy season. The rainy season, eh? Well, that'll be round about now.

You should be wary of persons presenting themselves as police officers. There have been instances of visitors becoming victims of theft, extortion or sexual assault by persons who may or may not be police officers. So forget 'when in doubt ask a policeman'?

Stay alert and do not travel alone. Oh dear.

I knew by now there was no use in dwelling on these overly cautious warnings, and as usual, it didn't seem anything like as bad as they made out. In fact, Guatemala struck me as a gentle, amiable sort of place. That is, until I hit the sprawling, seething fleshpot that is Guatemala City with its wretched shanty towns in the garbage dumps, tooled-up security men in blacked-out Jeeps and hopeless, shoeless children selling flowers, lighters and anything else they could find at the traffic lights. I didn't mean to go there, but the concept of ring roads hadn't made it to this part of the world, thus the CA–1 dived straight in and out of the savage heart of every Central American capital city. The 'in' bit was easy enough, but getting out on the other side was another matter.

'*Centro Americana Uno?* The road to El Salvador?' I shouted to the drivers of the cars beside me in the traffic, craning to hear their replies before the lights changed and they sped away with the combined roar of a hundred rotting exhausts, zig-zagging across each other's lanes in a billow of black smoke, horns blasting at everyone and everything in sight. This scene was repeated at every red light and, as usual, each of my enquiries elicited an array of fingers pointing in different directions, leading me on a distinctly un-merry dance around the city, searching helplessly for signs, clues, the casting of shadows, anything to guide me south through this hellish maze. The few road signs I saw referred to places that weren't even mentioned on my map and the infuriating one-way system sent me cavorting around the city centre in a dizzy spiral, fading fast under the tropical sun and the oppressive heat produced by the mobile metal prison of decrepit vehicles that penned me in on all sides.

'Uh-oh!' I groaned, feeling a little nudge to the back of the bike as one of my overstuffed pannier bags clipped the wing mirror of a car as I filtered through six lanes of stifling, grid-locked traffic. I stopped to apologise to the four women inside and was relieved to find I had escaped seven years of bad luck – no damage done, just a slight dislodging of the mirror. The driver reached out of her window and readjusted its position.

'*Disculpe*,' I said to her. Sorry.

She turned to acknowledge me and with a sinking heart I watched her face change as our eyes met and she spotted the Get Rich Quick scheme that had presented itself to her. Her passengers needed no prompting, they were on message, and raring to go.

Rolling down the windows, the four of them launched into an aggressive verbal attack, pointing at the mirror and waving their fists in a dramatic manner that would have been quite comical, had they not been deadly serious. I attempted to pacify them, showing them that their mirror had survived unscathed, but they didn't care to hear my opinion – this was their lucky day! The dollar signs were twinkling in their eyes like a Las Vegas fruit machine, and Ding! Ding! Ding!, they'd hit the jackpot. Their hysterical yelling knew no bounds, and although I couldn't make out what they were saying, the menacing tone told me all I needed to know.

'*No entiendo*,' I explained calmly. '*No hablo español*.'

But they continued to scream their furious diatribe at me.

'*No entiendo. Disculpe*.' I shrugged.

The discordant quartet turned low and more threatening, all the time shaking their heads in a slow ominous fashion. Big trouble in Guatemala City.

'*No entiendo*,' I repeated, enjoying the benefit of our linguistic stalemate, but they weren't giving in that easily. An English translation was attempted.

'Broke!' one of them screeched, pointing at the mirror.

'*Sí, sí*. Broke! You broke,' another agreed.

'*Dolares!* Dollars!' came a shrieked demand from the back seat.

I patiently showed them once again that the mirror was in good shape, nothing broken, I explained, I'd just knocked it out of position and they couldn't possibly begin to imagine how darned sorry I was that I had ever tangled with their bloody mirror and for crying out loud, would they please pipe down now?

'Broke!' they howled, playing up to the other drivers who were leaning out of their windows, watching the performance.

'*Disculpe!*' I protested through gritted teeth. I Am Sorry. 'Broke! Broke!' screamed the driver, her eyes slitty with rage.

I was confounded. The evidence was there for us all to see – the mirror was in full working order – but still they thought that if they screamed long enough and loud enough, their obviously false accusations would bear financial fruit. Their complete lack of rational thinking was quite bizarre. Upping the ante, they began motioning for me to pull over to the side of the road. I didn't know what they had in mind, maybe a hair-pulling contest or a spot of arm wrestling? One of the women in the back seat flung open the door and lunged out of the car, gesticulating manically and fussing over the mirror as if it was her firstborn child. I'd seen enough of their drama queen antics to realise that these chancers were nothing if not completely bonkers and that any argument based on reason would be totally lost on them.

'Broke! Money, fifty dollars!' the woman addressed me in

menacing tones, her face inches away from mine, jabbing at my arm with a sharp red fingernail. This was it; I'd had enough of these have-a-go housewife extortionists. I surveyed the deadlock of snarled-up vehicles ahead of me and laughed inwardly at the obvious simplicity of the solution.

'*Señoras* . . .' I addressed them collectively with the biggest, friendliest smile I could muster. Their eyes settled on me with suspicious steely anticipation, awaiting my announcement.

'. . . UP YOURS!' And with a flick of the middle finger, I was out of there, throttle wide open, bombing it through the stationary cars, weaving in and out of the gaps to the front of the queue, running the red light, over the junction, through the tangle of buses and cars, through another red, horns blaring, down a side road, up a one-way street, never looking back. Once I was sure I'd shaken off the opportunist harridans, I allowed myself a sigh of relief and an affectionate pat for the nippy Serow.

'Now *that* is why you ride a motorcycle,' I said to myself with a grin.

I continued my tour of the city, searching more avidly than ever for that southbound escape route.

Eventually I saw it: a road sign marked CA–1. Oh joy! Thank you, thank you, God of Motorcycling, get me out of this labyrinth of grot! But relief soon gave way to dread when I felt a strange sense of déjà vu creeping up on me. Hadn't I passed that building with the fountains before? And that gas station looks awfully familiar . . . but weren't they on the other side of the road last time I saw them? My sense of direction had become so utterly addled that although I was indeed heading out of the city on the CA–1, it was back the way I'd come in. Now I had to start the nightmare all over again! I pulled into the petrol station and looked up the word for 'lost' in my dictionary, completely frazzled by my geographical disorder.

'*Zona* 1, very dangerous, do not go there,' warned the gas station attendant, in response to my plea for directions.

'Yes,' I replied wearily, 'I've just spent an hour riding around there, now please, can you tell me—'

'Six people killed every day in Guatemala City,' he interrupted in earnest tones.

'Yes, yes, jolly good,' I said impatiently, 'but I'm actually looking to get out of here—'

'They stop you, they want money, and bang bang!' he said, imitating a gun held up against his head.

'Yeah, I can believe it,' I replied.

The shelves of the little shop were crammed with bottles of oil, exhaust repair bandage and lots of other bits and bobs for the Guatemalan boy racer. But there was a distinct lack of maps. Yet another idea, along with road signs and ring roads, that hadn't caught on in this neck of the woods.

After a while the realisation dawned on me that this man didn't actually have any of the answers, he was just idling away the day with his conversational horror stories, so, none the wiser, I returned to the fray for another gruelling lap. Once I'd established that I could now identify all the flags outside the embassy buildings, had translated and memorised the anti-USA graffiti in the underpass (BUSH GENOSIDA, ENEMIGO DE LA HUMANIDAD) and ridden past the same newspaper seller so many times that I was beginning to consider him a close friend, I was forced to consider the possibility that in fact, my trip had come to its end. Forget Ushuaia, forget South America, forget everything. This was it; there was no way out of Guatemala

City. I was destined to spend the rest of my life riding round and round and round this infernal black hole.

Bzzzz went the sound of a tinted electric window retreating next to me.

'You need some help?' came the gentleman's voice from within the car in perfect, almost accentless English. Whatever he was driving was black, shiny and had personalised Guatemalan number plates. I peered inside to find an immaculately dressed man fixing me with a welcome friendly smile. A rich bouquet of expensive aftershave and leather upholstery rushed out with a whoosh of cool aircon. I felt very grubby and smelly all of a sudden.

'I'm trying to find the *Centro Americana*, towards the border with El Salvador,' I explained. How many times had I said these words today? I was sick of hearing them.

'Follow me,' he said, 'I will show you where the road leaves the city, then you just keep going, keep going and you come to the frontier.'

My guardian angel had arrived!

'And a piece of advice,' he added, 'if you ever need to ask for directions, you must stop the best cars, like this one.' He waved a gilded hand around the luxury interior. 'If someone in Guatemala is driving a car like this, they will certainly speak English, and may be a very important person, maybe someone who can help you, someone in a high position. Do you understand what I am saying?' He looked at me with a hint of a knowing smile.

'Er . . . right . . . thanks for the tip,' I said, totally confused by his subtlety.

'Or maybe . . . they are a drug dealer . . . HA HA!' He roared with laughter. 'Now, follow me.' The window buzzed shut as he disappeared behind the black glass.

I was past caring whether my mystery man was a coke baron or the president of Guatemala. Either way, I never found out. Good as his word, he left me on the edge of town with a glittering salute and disappeared back into the mean streets. The straggling outskirts of the city went on for miles in a blur of slums and industrial decay, before the highway finally broke away into open country and another international border loomed.

MIKE CARTER

Extract from

UNEASY RIDER

Mike Carter is a freelance travel writer. Originally serialised as a weekly diary column in the *Observer, Uneasy Rider* (2008) is the result of a rash, drunken, post-divorce-inspired promise to take a BMW R1200GS around the world and find out what the rest of his life held. Six months, 20,000 miles and twenty-seven countries later, this is a very funny, sensitive and honest contribution to the classic mid-life crisis genre.

From Cluj-Napoca I travelled south to Sighisoara, the afore-mentioned dreamy town with a perfectly preserved medieval citadel at its core and a neat and varied line in 'Vlad Tepes woz here' memorabilia. I rode up the steep cobbled ramp and through the gateway into the main square. It was packed with tour parties following guides with umbrellas and stalls selling Dracula masks and t-shirts.

I parked the bike and walked around for a while, down cobbled alleyways flanked by sixteenth-century burgher houses, past the massive clock tower, with its pageant of slowly revolving figurines, and up to an ancient church up on the hill, reached via an old stone staircase with a wooden roof along its entire span.

It was one of the most stunning towns I had ever seen. Sue and Joe would have loved it here, and I would have loved it there more had Sue and Joe been there.

I strolled back to the bike and sat astride it for a while, smoking, thinking, feeling a bit dislocated. The guy who looked after the car park walked over and said hello. He'd been admiring my bike, he said, rode one himself, and told me how he dreamed of hitting the road one day.

His name was Marc. He'd signed up for the Romanian secret service after leaving college 'thinking I'd be tracking people down on my motorbike', but he'd been put in an office in a suit where he typed up reports all day until he could stand it no longer and quit. Now he was looking after this car park until something came up and he could afford to take his road trip.

'But with the money I earn here, maybe this is something I never get to do,' he said, and held his shoulders in a shrug and turned his palms towards the sky. 'But I dream about it all the time. You are living my dreams. You are a very lucky man.'

Thirty-odd miles down the road from Sighisoara, I turned off the main road and followed a rutted, twisting track through a dense forest. My conversation with Marc had been a timely bucket of cold water. What I really wanted tonight was not another bar or nightclub, nor a swish hotel with all the amenities, nor the company of other travellers, nor a Dracula-themed restaurant, nor Aussie detectives shagging their way around the former Soviet bloc.

I wanted to take a dirt track, any dirt track, find a patch of ground, pitch my tent and, accompanied only by the bottle of vodka, the bread and the garlic sausage (it pays to be careful in these parts) I'd bought back in Sighisoara, gaze up at the stars and listen to the forest nightshift go about its work.

It had begun to rain again, with the odd low growl of thunder thrown in for the requisite Transylvanian ambience. Just as I was about to pull over and make camp, the forest ended and I emerged somewhere in the sixteenth century.

The main street of the Roma village – just hardened clay really, turning swiftly to mud – was full of horses, and oxen, pulling carts piled high with straw, the drivers in pork pie hats, ancient bolt-action rifles slung over their shoulders.

Wizened old Roma women in headscarves carried their

grandchildren on their backs in slings fashioned from rugs. There was a hand pump in the street from which villagers were drawing water. People sat out on their steps to watch this strange creature pass, and scruffy, shoeless urchins chased after me.

I felt a tad vulnerable, uncomfortable. Five years earlier, I had been in Romania's most cosmopolitan city imagining I was in mortal danger. Now I was in the middle of the forest, in the middle of nowhere and darkness closing in, and I was drawing a crowd, many of whom were armed. It's not easy to be inconspicuous riding a 1200cc motorcycle through a Brueghel painting.

I stopped and asked a man smoking a pipe if there was anywhere to stay in town. But he didn't speak English, so I made the palms together on the side of the head gesture and made a circular motion with my arm.

He shook his head with a perplexed look on his face, then beamed and said 'Da, da', and beckoned me into his house which had not looked like a bed and breakfast from the outside. For good reason, it would seem, for the next minute he was pointing to his sofa and then making the palms together on the side of the head gesture.

Before I knew what was happening, a succession of small boys were carrying my luggage into the room. Shortly after, the entire village came round to see the stranger. There was lots of giggling and nudging and I poured my vodka into small glass tumblers and chipped mugs and then I cut my sausage into slices with my Leatherman and offered it around.

But they weren't too keen on the sausage and instead the old woman of the house produced a steaming tureen of sour soup with pork and beans, and we slurped it and ate heavy, dark bread, and drank more vodka. They spoke Romanian and I spoke English and we seemed to get along just fine. Vodka makes polyglots of us all.

I went through my guidebook's conversations and essentials section and tried to ask my host in Romanian what his name was, but I don't think I pronounced it correctly as he kept pointing to his hat.

After dinner, I walked back on to the main street. The boys who had earlier carried my luggage were playing football in the moonlight. They invited me to join in and they raced around me, screaming.

The smallest boy fired a shot into the top left-hand corner of the barn door, only for it to be ruled offside by a consensus of boys whose chief arbitration qualifications seemed to revolve around the fact that they were the biggest. Arguments ensued, and pushing and shoving, and I produced a scrap of paper from my pocket and flourished it at the chief rabble rouser, who theatrically gesticulated with his arms and pulled his 'who, me?' face, and grabbed his shirt at chest height before looking to the heavens as if seeking divine arbitration.

I showed off my best moves, sending long balls down the line with the outside of my foot, selling dummies to ten-year olds with relish and trying to organise our midfield into a diamond formation, like grown-ups do who've forgotten the sheer joy of just chasing a ball. But the diamond thing never really took hold and I ended up just running aimlessly after the ball. For a magical few minutes, I actually forgot I wasn't 10 years old.

I turned like Ronaldo and then, like Ronaldo, fell flat on my face. It would have been a cynical foul, if anybody had been near me. The ball forgotten, the boys raced over to me en masse and bodily picked me up, 20 pairs of little hands patting me down like I was a man on fire, with gentle care and concern in their faces. Whether it was the dust, or the pain, or something else, I couldn't say, but after the free kick had been awarded, and I stepped aside to put my knees back in their sockets, I had the smallest of tears in my eye.

From Transylvania, I headed south on the Transfagarasan road, for bikers a legendary ribbon of tarmac crossing the high Fagaras Mountains, laid across the landscape as if by a giant hand drizzling black syrup from a giant spoon. It was built in the early seventies by Ceausescu, as part of his fanatical, megalomanic zeal to conquer nature. Of course, in the fine tradition of dictators, old Nicolae wasn't actually there getting his hands dirty. No, the thing with megalomanic zeal is that it tends to keep a man tied up in the office.

The Transfagarasan started gently enough, flopping through rolling uplands of sheep-flecked meadows, past haystacks on sticks like upturned candyfloss. The greatest hazard was still the horse-drawn carts that outnumbered cars in the villages and, weirdly, Romanian geese that, unlike any other geese I'd encountered on the trip, seemed to have a personal issue with the engine pitch of a BMW R1200GS.

Some distance off I'd spot them pricking up their ears, or whatever it is that geese prick up, and start to spread their wings in an avian version of 'you wanna piece of me, huh?' By the time I drew alongside them, they would be in a right old flap, squawking and hissing and chasing me down the road. Once at a safe distance, I would pull over and watch other people on motorbikes pass by. Not a peep. Bizarre.

After about eight miles, the road began to sharply rise, and the turns grew more and more angular as I plunged through dense spruce forest. As I climbed, the trees started to first shrink and then disappear completely as I emerged at what felt like the roof of the world, with steep bluffs and foaming waterfalls and, even in midsummer, a white carpet of crisp snow. I had to keep flipping up my helmet to squeeze my nose and pop my ears, and eventually pulled over to dig out my fleece and thick riding gloves.

Through a mile-long tunnel blasted out of the rock and then more breathtaking views, a bleak granite moonscape, clouds bubbling rapidly over the incisor peaks above, the slenderest of margins at the side of the black strip separating the road from the abyss falling vertically away. There were few guard rails. Perhaps Nicolae considered them a bit effete.

There were plenty of shrines, though, and denuded clumps of flowers sitting next to weather-worn photographs of people who presumably were so taken with the views that they forgot to turn the wheel.

But the large number of traffic accidents might also have had something to do with the road surface, which was, to use the technical term, shit. The potholes were so numerous that at times the road resembled a Yorkshire pudding tray, some of them so large that they had people fishing in them. Polish people should come to Romania. They'd soon be feeling much better about their own roads.

I pulled over once again to drink it all in. Shadows from the clouds scudded down the valley. There was nothing save a deep, sonorous silence. A giant golden eagle soared high on the thermals.

I looked at my guidebook to see what it had to say about the Transfagarasan. Ahead of me, apparently, lay another 15 miles of clenched buttocks and white knuckles. There was also Lake Bâlea, which promised to 'hover like a mirror among the rocks' and, surprise, at Poienari, a castle that was regarded as the real-deal, no-doubt-about-it, accept-no-imitations, you've-tried-the-rest-now-try-the-best, roll-up-and-get-your-T-shirt Dracula's castle. Who was this Vlad character? George Wimpey in a cloak?

The road plunged down the other side of the mountain in a sweep of hairpins the profile of a Jeffrey Archer lie detector test.

With 11 weeks and 9,000 miles of motorcycling under my tyres, I decided it was time to test my skills to the limit. I gunned towards the turns, at 40, 50, 60 miles per hour, my heart in my mouth. I picked the racing line, whatever that was, touched ever so gently on my front brake, shifted my bum to the inside of the saddle, and leaned in.

I remembered Kevin Sanders telling me about an advanced turning technique, where you push the handlebars in the opposite direction to the turn, just like a speedway rider, and the bike gyroscopically tries to fall to the floor.

Perhaps on top of a mountain, on a road full of potholes, with no guard rails, sheer drops and a long ambulance ride to the nearest A&E, this wasn't the wisest place to practise being Valentino Rossi. But it worked beautifully as I became one with the BMW, and with the road, flying round the hairpins, the experience akin to dancing with a supremely gifted partner. I felt my boot catch the road as I banked into a turn, and the wheels slip ever so slightly, and I imagined my rapidly disappearing chicken strips – the worn/unworn edge of the tyre that's a telltale of your hardcore/wimp style as a rider – affording me plenty of kudos with the very baddest biker dudes.

I was riding to the limit of my ability, one tiny error of judgement could have brought catastrophe and the ensuing sickening crunching noise followed by the silence and the stillness before the pain would start to rise and rise. But these thoughts only made me want to ride faster, hooked on the sensation of being on the edge, a delicious glimpse of utter freedom, total peace.

I approached a bend. Fast. I couldn't see the exit. It was tight, and as I leaned into it, it got tighter and tighter. I couldn't touch the brakes. On a road like this, with loose shale on the surface, and potholes everywhere, it could have been fatal, my wheels falling away from under me. This is one of the most common causes of death on a motorbike: misjudging your speed coming into a bend.

I started to drift across the road, unable to keep in my lane. The bend showed no signs of opening up, smoothing out. On the far side of the road were spruce trees. I looked at them. There was one in particular, thicker than the rest. I stared at it. The bike started to straighten, move upright. I headed for the tree. I went to hit the brakes. I was going to crash, no doubt, but any reduction in speed might make all the difference. The whole thing had taken perhaps less than a couple of seconds, but somehow time was stretched.

I remembered Kevin's words. Have faith. Look where you want to go. The bike will follow. It has to.

I ripped my eyes from the spruce tree. It was an act of will. And I turned my head to look at the bend once more. The bike dipped again, leaned in. I think I left the road at one stage, crossing the line on the far side, riding over needles and cones, trees flashing past. But I couldn't be sure, because all I was looking at was the road ahead, the bend opening up, my right hand twisting back the throttle, me whooping like a lunatic.

'The fine will be eight million lei,' the police officer was saying to me.

'But that's . . . that's about 200 euros,' I replied, which a quick calculation told me was roughly the average Romanian wage for a month. I could feel my bottom lip trembling.

'You should not go so fast. This road very dangerous,' he said.

'I'm sorry.'

'No good. You under arrest. You get in car and we go to bank to pay.'

I felt like the victim of a cashpoint mugging.

He ordered me to leave my bike by the side of the road and get into the passenger seat of the police car. Then we drove away heading for God knows where. After about 10 minutes, down a quiet country lane, the officer pulled over into a lay-by. Unless there was an ATM in one of the adjacent oak trees, which I was pretty certain there was not, I was guessing that this wasn't the end of the journey.

The officer switched off the ignition, slowly, deliberately, and turned to me, his gun nestling against his thigh.

'Okay. For you, for lei cash, there is 20 per cent discount,' he said.

'Discount?'

'Yes. Consider it gesture of goodwill from the kind Romanian people.'

As he was talking, he was fishing around in his wallet. He pulled out some photographs. My prejudices started to resurface. I imagined they might be of bloodstained cells, or show corpses lying face down besides a lay-by, this lay-by . . .

'This my sister, she live London,' he said, showing me a picture of a smiling woman toasting the camera with a large glass of red wine.

'You married?'

'No.'

'I give you her address. She is very nice. Make good wife.'

'I'm not looking for a wife,' I said to him.

'You no like my sister?' he said.

'It's not that, it's . . .'

'How about this one?' He'd pulled another picture out. 'She live Coventry.'

'She seems very nice, too . . . Look, I'm flattered you think I might be good enough for your sisters, but I'm not interested . . .'

'Thirty per cent?'

'What?'

'Discount. Thirty per cent, as goodwill and because you think my sisters very nice.'

I laughed.

'What would the discount be if I married one of your sisters?' I said.

The policeman suddenly looked at me solemnly, gravely.

'Mister. You try bribe Romanian police officer? Is very serious offence.'

At that point I remembered something someone had told me before I left England, about the police in Romania. Possibly Pub Guy, with his PhD in Ukrainian Visa Regulations. Whoever it was had told me about the dodgy Romanian police, about the last vestiges of the once-endemic corruption and how it was being clamped down on as the country moved towards EU membership and how, if you get pulled over, you should always insist on going to the police station and getting a receipt.

'I think we should go to the police station,' I said. 'I will need a receipt for the ticket.'

For a second, a melancholy filled the policeman's eyes, as if recalling a lost, glorious age, a time when he'd been king.

Then he put away the photographs and we drove off, slowly, in silence, to the police station, where I got a receipt for the 30-euro fine.

HUNTER S. THOMPSON

SONG OF THE SAUSAGE CREATURE

Hunter S. Thompson was born in Louisville, Kentucky in
1937. A flamboyant, renegade journalist, his style of
experiencing the action itself and studying the effect on
himself often meant that he became a central figure within
his own writing; this has come to be known as *gonzo*
journalism.

Thompson was fond of the incendiary combination of
drugs, alcohol and firearms which often resulted in the
chaos and disorder which were seemingly to typify his life.
However he subsequently claimed in an interview that
maybe things were not quite always what they seemed and
perhaps he'd embellished the mayhem.

A sports, cultural and political journalist, he was also
the author of classic cult, counterculture work and is best
known for his first book, *Hell's Angels* (1966).

Thompson committed suicide in 2005 aged 67.

There are some things nobody needs in this world, and a bright-red, hunchback, warp-speed 900cc café racer is one of them – but I want one anyway, and on some days I actually believe I need one. That is why they are dangerous.

Everybody has fast motorcycles these days. Some people go 150 miles an hour on two-lane blacktop roads, but not often. There are too many oncoming trucks and too many radar cops and too many stupid animals in the way. You have to be a little crazy to ride these super-torque high-speed crotch rockets anywhere except a racetrack – and even there, they will scare the whimpering shit out of you . . . There is, after all, not a pig's eye worth of difference between going head-on into a Peterbilt or sideways into the bleachers. On some days you get what you want, and on others, you get what you need.

When *Cycle World* called me to ask if I would road-test the new Harley Road King, I got uppity and said I'd rather have a Ducati superbike. It seemed like a chic decision at the time, and my friends on the superbike circuit got very excited. 'Hot damn,' they said. 'We will take it to the track and blow the bastards away.'

'Balls,' I said. 'Never mind the track. The track is for punks. We are Road People. We are Café Racers.'

The Café Racer is a different breed, and we have our own situations. Pure speed in sixth gear on a 5,000-foot straightaway is one thing, but pure speed in third gear on a gravel-strewn downhill ess-turn is quite another.

But we like it. A thoroughbred Café Racer will ride all night through a fog storm in freeway traffic to put himself into what somebody told him was the ugliest and tightest diminishing-radius loop turn since Genghis Khan invented the corkscrew.

Café Racing is mainly a matter of taste. It is an atavistic mentality, a peculiar mix of low style, high speed, pure dumbness, and overweening commitment to the *Café Life* and all its dangerous pleasures . . . I am a Café Racer myself, on some days – and it is one of my finest addictions . . .

I am not without scars on my brain and my body, but I can live with them. I still feel a shudder in my spine every time I see a picture of a Vincent Black Shadow, or when I walk into a public restroom and hear crippled men whispering about the terrifying Kawasaki Triple . . . I have visions of compound femur-fractures and large black men in white hospital suits holding me down on a gurney while a nurse called 'Bess' sews the flaps of my scalp together with a stitching drill.

Ho, ho. Thank God for these flashbacks. The brain is such a wonderful instrument (until God sinks his teeth into it). Some people hear Tiny Tim singing when they go under, and others hear the song of the Sausage Creature.

When the Ducati turned up in my driveway, nobody knew what to do with it. I was in New York, covering a polo tournament, and people had threatened my life. My lawyer said I should give myself up and enroll in the Federal Witness Protection Program. Other people said it had something to do with the polo crowd, or maybe Ron Ziegler.

The motorcycle business was the last straw. It had to be the work of my enemies, or people who wanted to hurt me. It was the vilest kind of bait, and they knew I would go for it.

Of course. You want to cripple the bastard? Send him a 160-mph café-racer. And include some license plates, so he'll think it's a streetbike. He's queer for anything fast.

Which is true. I have been a connoisseur of fast motorcycles all my life. I bought a brand-new 650 BSA Lightning when it was billed as 'the fastest motorcycle ever tested by *Hot Rod* magazine.' I have ridden a 500-pound Vincent through traffic on the Ventura Freeway with burning oil on my legs and run the Kawa 750 Triple through Beverly Hills at night with a head full of acid . . . I have ridden with Sonny Barger and smoked weed in biker bars with Jack Nicholson, Grace Slick and my infamous old friend, Ken Kesey, a legendary Café Racer.

Some people will tell you that slow is good – and it may be, on some days – but I am here to tell you that fast is better. I've always believed this, in spite of the trouble it's caused me. Being shot out of a cannon will always be better than being squeezed out of a tube. That is why God made fast motorcycles, Bubba . . .

So when I got back from the U.S. Open Polo Championship in New York and found a fiery red rocket-style bike in my garage, I realized I was back in the road-testing business.

The brand-new Ducati 900 *Campione del Mundo Desmodue* Supersport double-barrelled magnum Café Racer filled me with feelings of lust every time I looked at it. Others felt the same way. My garage quickly became a magnet for drooling superbike groupies. They quarrelled and bitched at each other about who would be first to help me evaluate my new toy . . . And I did, of course, need a certain spectrum of opinions, besides my own, to properly judge this motorcycle. The Woody Creek Perverse Environmental Testing Facility is a long way from Daytona or even top-fuel challenge sprints on the Pacific Coast Highway, where teams of big-bore Kawasakis and Yamahas are said to race head-on against each other in death-defying games of 'chicken' at 100 miles an hour . . .

No. Not everybody who buys a high-dollar torque-brute yearns to go out in a ball of fire on a public street in L.A. Some of us are decent people who want to stay out of the emergency room but still blast through neo-gridlock traffic in residential districts whenever we feel like it . . . For that we need Fine Machinery.

Which we had – no doubt about that. The Ducati people in New Jersey had opted, for reasons of their own, to send me the 900SP for testing – rather than their 916 crazy-fast, state-of-the-art superbike track-racer. It was far too fast, they said – and prohibitively expensive – to farm out for testing to a gang of half-mad Colorado cowboys who think they're world-class Café Racers.

The Ducati 900 *is* a finely engineered machine. My neighbours called it beautiful and admired its racing lines. The nasty little bugger looked like it was going 90 miles an hour when it was standing still in my garage.

Taking it on the road, though, was a genuinely terrifying experience. I had no sense of speed until I was going 90 and coming up fast on a bunch of pickup trucks going into a wet curve along the river. I went for both brakes, but only the front one worked, and I almost went end over end. I was out of control staring at the tailpipe of a U.S. Mail truck, still stabbing frantically at my rear brake pedal, which I just couldn't find . . . I am too tall for these new-age roadracers; they are not built for any rider taller than five-nine, and the rearset brake pedal was not where I thought it would be. Mid-size Italian pimps who like to race from one café to another on the boulevards of Rome in a flat-line prone position might like this, but I do not.

I was hunched over the tank like a person diving into a pool that got emptied yesterday. Whacko! Bashed on the concrete bottom, flesh ripped off, a Sausage Creature with no teeth, fucked-up for the rest of its life.

We all love Torque, and some of us have taken it straight over the high side from time to time – and there is always pain in that . . . But there is also Fun, the deadly element, and Fun is what you get when you screw this monster on. BOOM! Instant take-off, no screeching or squawking around like a fool with your teeth clamping down on your tongue and your mind completely empty of everything but fear.

No. This bugger digs right in and shoots you straight down the pipe, for good or ill.

On my first take-off, I hit second gear and went through the speed limit on a two-lane blacktop highway full of ranch traffic. By the time I went up to third, I was going 75 and the tach was barely above 4,000 rpm . . .

And that's when it got its second wind. From 4,000 to 6,000 in third will take you from 75 mph to 95 in two seconds – and after that, Bubba, you still have fourth, fifth, and sixth. Ho, ho.

I never got to sixth gear, and I didn't get deep into fifth. This is a shameful admission for a full-bore Café Racer, but let me tell you something, old sport: This motorcycle is simply too goddamn fast to ride at speed in any kind of normal road traffic unless you're ready to go straight down the centreline with your nuts on fire and a silent scream in your throat.

When aimed in the right direction at high speed, though, it has unnatural capabilities. This I unwittingly discovered as I made my approach to a sharp turn across some railroad tracks, and saw that I was going way too fast and that my only chance was to veer right and screw it on totally, in a desperate attempt to leapfrog the curve by going airborne.

It was a bold and reckless move, but it was necessary. And it worked: I felt like Evel Knievel as I soared across the tracks with the rain in my eyes and my jaws clamped together in fear. I tried to spit down on the tracks as I passed them, but my mouth was too dry . . . I landed hard on the edge of the road and lost my grip for a moment as the Ducati began fishtailing crazily into oncoming traffic. For two or three seconds I came face to face with the Sausage Creature . . .

But somehow the brute straightened out. I passed a schoolbus on the right and got the bike under control long enough to gear down and pull off into an abandoned gravel driveway where I stopped and turned off the engine. My hands had seized up like claws and the rest of my body was numb. I went into a trance for 30 or 40 seconds until I was finally able to light a cigarette and calm down enough to ride home. I was too hysterical to shift gears, so I went the whole way in first at 40 miles an hour.

Whoops! What am I saying? Tall stories, ho, ho . . . We are motorcycle people; we walk tall and we laugh at whatever's funny. We shit on the chests of the Weird . . .

But when we ride very fast motorcycles, we ride with immaculate sanity. We might abuse a substance here and there, but only when it's right. The final measure of any rider's skill is the inverse ratio of his preferred Travelling Speed to the number of bad scars on his body. It is that simple: If you ride fast and crash, you are a bad rider. And if you are a bad rider, you should not ride motorcycles.

The emergence of the superbike has heightened this equation

drastically. Motorcycle technology has made such a great leap forward. Take the Ducati. You want optimum cruising speed on this bugger? Try 90mph in fifth at 5,500 rpm – and just then, you see a bull moose in the middle of the road. WHACKO. Meet the Sausage Creature.

Or maybe not: The Ducati 900 is so finely engineered and balanced and torqued that you *can* do 90 mph in fifth through a 35-mph zone and get away with it. The bike is not just fast – it is *extremely* quick and responsive, and it *will* do amazing things . . . It is like riding the original Vincent Black Shadow, which would outrun an F-86 jet fighter on the take-off runway, but at the end, the F-86 would go airborne and the Vincent would not, and there was no point in trying to turn it. WHAMMO! The Sausage Creature strikes again.

There is a fundamental difference, however, between the old Vincents and the new breed of superbikes. If you rode the Black Shadow at top speed for any length of time, you would almost certainly die. That is why there are not many life members of the Vincent Black Shadow Society. The Vincent was like a bullet that went straight; the Ducati is like the magic bullet in Dallas that went sideways and hit JFK and the Governor of Texas at the same time.

It was impossible. But so was my terrifying sideways leap across the railroad tracks on the 900SP. The bike did it easily with the grace of a fleeing tomcat. The landing was so easy I remember thinking, Goddamnit, if I had screwed it on a little more I could have gone a lot farther.

Maybe this is the new Café Racer macho. My bike is so much faster than yours that I dare you to ride it, you lame little turd. Do you have the balls to ride this BOTTOMLESS PIT OF TORQUE?

That is the attitude of the new-age superbike freak, and I am one of them. On some days they are about the most fun you can have with your clothes on. The Vincent just killed you a lot faster than a superbike will. A fool couldn't ride the Vincent Black Shadow more than once, but a fool can ride a Ducati 900 many times, and it will always be a bloodcurdling kind of fun. That is the Curse of Speed which has plagued me all my life. I am a slave to it. On my tombstone they will carve, IT NEVER GOT FAST ENOUGH FOR ME.

THOM GUNN

THE UNSETTLED MOTORCYCLIST'S VISION OF HIS DEATH

Thom Gunn was born in Kent in 1929. His parents, both strong personalities with successful careers in journalism, divorced when he was ten years old. Tragically his adored mother committed suicide in 1943, an event Gunn later recorded in his poem *The Gas Poker*.

After a period of National Service Gunn went on to study English Literature at Trinity College, Cambridge where he came under the influence of F.R. Leavis. Having graduated in 1953, his first verse collection was published in 1954 to critical acclaim. The same year he took up a place at Stanford University teaching Creative Writing where he could also maintain his relationship with his partner, Mike Kitay. He went on to teach largely part-time at Berkeley College in California where the bohemian lifestyle suited his character, and he was regarded as a charismatic lecturer with an enthusiastic following.

Best known for his poetry of which the finest collections are probably *The Sense of Movement* (1957) and *The Man With Night Sweats* (1992), Thom Gunn died in San Francisco in 2004 aged 74 of substance abuse.

Across the open countryside,
Into the walls of rain I ride.
It beats my cheek, drenches my knees,
But I am being what I please.

The firm heath stops, and marsh begins.
Now we're at war: whichever wins
My human will cannot submit
To nature, though brought out of it.
The wheels sink deep; the clear sound blurs:
Still, bent on the handle-bars,
I urge my chosen instrument
Against the mere embodiment.
The front wheel wedges fast between
Two shrubs of glazed insensate green
– Gigantic order in the rim
Of each flat leaf. Black eddies brim
Around my heel which, pressing deep,
Accelerates the waking sleep.

I used to live in sound, and lacked
Knowledge of still or creeping fact,
But now the stagnant strips my breath,
Leant on my cheek in weight of death.
Though so oppressed I find I may,
Through substance move. I pick my way
Where death and life in one combine,
Through the dark earth that is not mine,
Crowded with fragments, blunt, unformed;
While past my ear where noises swarmed
The marsh plant's white extremities.
Slow without patience, spread at ease
Invulnerable and soft, extend
With a quiet grasping towards their end.

And though the tubers, once I rot,
Reflesh my bones with pallid knot,
Till swelling out my clothes they feign
This dummy is a man again,
It is as servants they insist,
Without volition that they twist;
And habit does not leave them tired,
By men laboriously acquired.
Cell after cell the plants convert
My special richness in the dirt;
All that they get, they get by chance.

And multiply in ignorance.

THOMAS McGUANE

ME AND MY BIKE AND WHY

Thomas McGuane was born in Wyandotte, Michigan in
1939. He has written ten novels, the best known of which
is *Ninety-Two in the Shade* (1973), screenplays such as
The Missouri Breaks and *Tom Horn*, as well as a number
of collections of essays from one of which, *An Outside
Chance*, the following extract has been taken. It tells of
an impulsive purchase of a Matchless 500cc motorcycle
and conveys what so many of us will have felt when first
receiving the keys to our inexplicable desire but lacking
the sublime skill to put it down in writing with such
effortless charm, skill and humour.

Like many who buy a motorcycle, there had been for me the problem of getting over the rather harrowing insurance statistics as to just what it is that is likely to happen to you. Two years in California – a familiar prelude to acts of excess – had made of me an active motorcycle spectator. I watched and identified, finally resorting to bikers' magazines; and evolved a series of foundationless prejudices.

Following the war, motorcycling left a peculiar image in the national consciousness: porcine individuals wearing a sort of yachting cap with a white vinyl bill, the decorative braid pulled up over the hat; their motorcycles plated monsters, white rubber mud flaps studded with ruby stars hung from both fenders. Where are those machines now? Surely Andy Warhol can't have bought them all. Not every one of them is a decorative planter in a Michigan truck garden. But wherever they are, it is certain that the ghosts of cretinism collect close around the strenuously baroque plumbing of those inefficient engines and speak to us of an America that has gone.

It was easy for me initially to deplore the big road bikes, the motorcycles of the police and Hell's Angels. But finally even these 'hogs' and show bikes had their appeal, and sometimes I had dark fantasies of myself on El Camino Real, hands hung overhead from the big chopper bars, feet in front on weirdly automotive pedals, making all the decent people say: 'There goes one.'

I did it myself. Heading into San Francisco with my wife, our Land Rover blaring wide open at 52 miles per, holding up a quarter mile of good people behind us, people who didn't see why anybody needed four-wheel drive on the Bayshore Freeway, we ourselves would from time to time see a Lonesome Angel or Coffin Cheater or Satan's Slave or Gypsy Joker on his big chopper and say (either my wife or myself, together sometimes): 'There goes one.'

Anyway, it was somewhere along in here that I saw I was not that type, and began to think of sporting machines, even racing machines, big ones, because I had no interest in starting small and working my way up as I had been urged to do. I remember that I had told the writer Wallace Stegner what I intended, and he asked, 'Why do you people do this when you come to California?'

'It's like skiing,' I said, purely on speculation.

'Oh, yeah? What about the noise?'

But no one could stop me.

There was the dire question of money that ruled out many I saw. The English-built Triumph Metisse road racer was out of the question, for example. Some of the classics I found and admired – Ariel Square Fours, Vincent Black Shadows, BSA Gold Stars, Velocette Venoms or Phantom Clubmen, Norton Manxes – had to be eliminated on grounds of cost or outlandish maintenance problems.

Some of the stranger Japanese machinery, two-cycle, rotary-valved engines, I dismissed because they sounded funny. The Kawasaki Samurai actually seemed refined, but I refused to consider it. I had a corrupt Western ideal of a bike's exhaust rap, and the tuned megaphone exhausts of the Japanese motorcycles sounded like something out of the next century, weird loon cries of Oriental speed tuning.

*   *   *

There is a blurred moment in my head, a scenario of compulsion. I am in a motorcycle shop that is going out of business. I am writing a cheque that challenges the contents of my bank account. I am given ownership papers substantiated by the state of California, a crash helmet, and five gallons of fuel. Some minutes later I am standing beside my new motorcycle, sick all over. The man who sold it to me stares palely through the Thermopane window covered with the decals of the noble marques of 'performance.' He wonders why I have not moved.

I have not moved because I do not know what to do. I wish to advance upon the machine with authority but cannot. He would not believe I could have bought a motorcycle of this power without knowing so much as how to start its engine. Presently he loses interest and looks for another tormented creature in need of a motorcycle.

Unwatched, I can really examine the bike. Since I have no notion of how to operate it, it is purely an *objet*. I think of a friend with a road racer on a simple mahoghany block in front of his fireplace, except that he rides his very well.

The bike was rather beautiful. I suppose it still is. The designation, which now seems too cryptic for my taste, was 'Matchless 500,' and it was the motorcycle I believed I had thought up myself. It is a trifle hard to describe the thing to the uninitiated, but, briefly, it had a 500cc, one cylinder engine – a 'big single' in the patois of bike freaks – and an eloquently simple maroon teardrop-shaped tank that is as much the identifying mark on a Matchless, often otherwise unrecognizable through modification, as the chevron of a redwing blackbird. The front wheel, delicate as a bicycle's, carried a Dunlop K70 tyre (said to 'cling') and had no fender; a single cable led to the pale machined brake drum. Over the knobbly rear wheel curved an extremely brief magnesium fender with, instead of the lush buddy-seat of the fat motorcycles, a minute pillion of leather. The impression was of performance and of complete disregard for comfort. The equivalent in automobiles would be, perhaps, the Morgan, in sailboats the Finn.

I saw all of these things at once (remember the magazines I had been reading, the Ford Clymer books I had checked out of the library), and in that sense my apprehension of the motorcycle was perfectly literary. I still didn't know how to start it. Suddenly it looked big and mean and vicious and no fun at all.

I didn't want to experiment on El Camino Real, and moreover, it had begun to rain heavily. I had made up my mind to wheel it home, and there to peruse the operation manual, whose infuriating British locutions the Land Rover manual had prepared me for.

I was surprised at the sheer initial weight of the thing; it leaned towards me and pressed against my hip insistently all the way to the house. I was disturbed that a machine whose place in history seemed so familiar should look utterly foreign at close range. The fact that the last number on the speedometer was 140 seemed irresponsible.

It was dark by the time I got home. I wheeled it through the back gate and down the sidewalk through a yard turned largely to mud. About halfway to the kitchen door, I somehow got the thing tilted away from myself, and it slowly but quite determinedly toppled over in the mud, with me, gnashing, on top of it.

My wife came to the door and peered into the darkness. 'Tom?' I refused to vouchsafe an answer. I lay there in the mud, no longer struggling, as the spring rains of the San Francisco peninsula singled me out for special treatment. I was already composing the ad in the *Chronicle* that motorcycle people dream of finding: 'Big savings on Matchless 500. Never started by present owner. A real crown puff.' My wife threw on the porch light and perceived my discomfiture.

The contretemps had the effect of quickly getting us over the surprise that I had bought the motorcycle, questions of authorization, and so on. I headed for the showers. Scraped and muddy, I had excited a certain amount of pity. 'I'll be all right.'

No one told me to retard the spark. True enough, it was in the manual, but I had been unable to read that attentively. It had no plot, no characters. So my punishment was this: when I jumped on the kick starter, it backfired and more or less threw me off the bike. I was limping all through the first week from vicious blowbacks. I later learned it was a classic way to get a spiral fracture. I tried jumping lightly on the kick starter and, unfairly, it would blast back as viciously as with a sharp kick. Eventually it started, and sitting on it, I felt the torque tilt the bike under me. I was afraid to take my hands off the handlebars. My wife lowered the helmet onto my head; I compared it to the barber's basin Don Quixote had worn into battle, the Helmet of Mambrino.

I slipped my toe under the gearshift lever, lifted it into first, released the clutch, and magically glided away and made all my shifts through fourth, at which time I was on Sand Hill Road and going 50, my shirt in a soft air bubble at my back, my Levi's wrapped tight to my shins, my knuckles whitening under the giddy surge of pure undetained motion as I climbed gently into the foothills towards Los Altos. The road got more and more winding as I ascended, briskly but conservatively. Nothing in the air was lost on me as I passed through zones of smell and temperature as palpable transitions, running through sudden warm spots on the road where a single redwood 100 feet away had fallen and let in a shaft of sunlight. The road seemed tremendously spacious. The sound was behind me, so that when I came spiraling down out of the mountains and saw some farm boy had walked out to the side of the road to watch me go by, I realized he had heard me coming for a long time. And I wondered a little about the racket.

These rides became habitual and presumably more competent. I often rode up past La Honda for a view of the sea at the far edge of a declining cascade of manzanita-covered hills, empty and foggy. The smell of ocean was so perfectly evocative in a landscape divided among ranches and truck gardens whose pumpkins in the foggy air seemed to have an uncanny brilliance. A Japanese nursery stood along the road in clouds of tended vines on silver redwood lattice. I went past it to the sea and before riding home took a long walk on the ribbed, immense beach.

A fascinating aspect of the pursuit, not in the least bucolic, was the bike shop where one went for mechanical service, and which was a meeting place for the bike people, whose machines were poised out front in carefully conceived rest positions. At first, of course, no one would talk to me, but my motorcycle ideas were theirs; I was not riding one of the silly mechanisms that purred down the highway in a parody of the equipment these people lived for.

One day an admired racing mechanic – 'a good wrench' – came out front and gave my admittedly well-cared-for Matchless the once-over. He announced that it was 'very sanitary.' I was relieved. The fear, of course, is that he will tell you, 'The bike is wrong.'

'Thank you,' I said modestly. He professed himself an admirer of the 'Matchbox,' saying it was 'fairly rapid' and had enough torque to 'pull stumps.' Ultimately, I was taken in, treated kindly, and given the opportunity to ride some of the machinery that so excited me: the 'truly potent' Triumph Metisse, an almost uncontrollable supercharged Norton Atlas from New Mexico, and a couple of road-racing machines with foot pegs way back by the rear sprocket and stubby six-inch handlebars – so that you lay out on the bike and divide a sea of wind with the point of your chin.

One day I 'got off on the pavement,' that is, crashed. It was not much of a crash. I went into a turn too fast and ran off the shoulder and got a little 'road burn' requiring symbolic bandages at knees and elbows. I took the usual needling from the crew at the bike shop, and with secret pleasure accepted the temporary appellation, 'Crash Cargo.' I began taking dawn trips over the mountains to Santa Cruz, sometimes with others, sometimes alone, wearing a wool hunting shirt against the chill and often binoculars and an Audobon field guide.

Then one day I was riding in my own neighbourhood when a man made a U-turn in front of me and stopped, blocking the road. It was too late to brake and I had to put the bike down, riding it like a sled as it screeched across the pavement. It ran into the side of the car and I slid halfway under, the seat and knees torn out of my pants, scraped and bruised but without serious injury. I had heard the sharp clicking of my helmet against the pavement and later saw the depressions that might have been in my skull.

The man got out, accusing me of going 100 miles an hour, accusing me of being a Hell's Angel, and finally admitting he had been daydreaming and had not looked up the street before making his illegal manoeuvre. The motorcycle was a mess. He pleaded with me not to have physical injuries. He said he had very little insurance. And a family. 'Have a heart.'

'You ask this of a Hell's Angel?'

At the motorcycle shop I was urged to develop non-specific spinal trouble. A special doctor was named. But I had the motorcycle minimally repaired and sent the man the bill. When the settlement came, his name was at the top of the stationery. He was the owner of the insurance agency.

Perhaps it was the point-blank view from below of rocker panels and shock absorbers and the specious concern of the insurance man for my health that gave my mortality its little twinge. I suddenly did not want to get off on the pavement anymore or bring my road burn to the shop under secret bandages. I no longer cared if my bike was rapid and sanitary. I wanted to sell it, and I wanted to get out of California.

I did both these things, and in that order. But sometimes, in the midst of more tasteful activities, I miss the mournful howl of that big single engine as it came up on the cam, dropped revs, and started over on a new ratio; the long banking turns with the foot pegs sparking against the pavement and the great crocodile's tears the wind caused to trickle out from under my flying glasses. I'm behind a sensible windshield now, and the soaring curve of acceleration does not come up through the seat of my pants. I have an FM radio, and the car doesn't get bad mileage.

ROBERT M. PIRSIG

Extract from

ZEN AND THE ART OF MOTORCYCLE MAINTENANCE

Robert M. Pirsig was born in Minneapolis in 1928.
A writer and philosopher, Pirsig wrote his most famous
book, *Zen and the Art of Motorcycle Maintenance*, as an
account of a motorcycle journey he undertook with his
son, Chris, from Minneapolis to San Francisco. The bike
is not clearly identified but from photographs is thought
to have been a 1964 CB77 Honda 305cc Super Hawk.
Almost impossible to categorise, and famously rejected by
121 publishers before being taken on by William Morrow,
Zen has become a classic and has gone on to sell over
five million copies, making it probably the highest selling
work of philosophy.

The road winds on and on . . . we stop for rests and lunch, exchange small talk, and settle down to the long ride. The beginning fatigue of afternoon balances the excitement of the first day and we move steadily, not fast, not slow.

We have picked up a southwest side wind, and the cycle cants into the gusts, seemingly by itself, to counter the effect. Lately there's been a sense of something peculiar about this road, apprehension about something, as if we were being watched or followed. But there is not a car anywhere ahead, and in the mirror are only John and Sylvia way behind.

We are not in the Dakotas yet, but the broad fields show we are getting nearer. Some of them are blue with flax blossoms moving in long waves like the surface of the ocean. The sweep of the hills is greater than before and they now dominate every-thing else, except the sky, which seems wider. Farmhouses in the distance are so small we can hardly see them. The land is beginning to open up.

There is no one place or sharp line where the Central Plains end and the Great Plains begin. It's a gradual change like this that catches you unawares, as if you were sailing out from a choppy coastal harbour, noticed that the waves had taken on a deep swell, and turned back to see that you were out of sight of land. There are fewer native trees here and suddenly I am aware they are no longer native. They have been brought here and planted around houses and between fields in rows to break up the wind. But where they haven't been planted there is no underbrush, no second-growth saplings – only grass, sometimes with wildflowers and weeds, but mostly grass. This is grassland now. We are on the prairie.

I have a feeling none of us fully understands what four days on this prairie in July will be like. Memories of car trips across them are always of flatness and great emptiness as far as you can see, extreme monotony and boredom as you drive for hour after hour, getting nowhere, wondering how long this is going to last without a turn in the road, without a change in the land going on and on to the horizon.

John was worried Sylvia would not be up to the discomfort of this and planned to have her fly to Billings, Montana, but Sylvia and I both talked him out of it. I argued that physical discomfort is important only when the mood is wrong. Then you fasten on to whatever thing is uncomfortable and call that the cause. But if the mood is right, then physical discomfort doesn't mean much. And when thinking about Sylvia's moods and feelings, I couldn't see her complaining.

Also, to arrive in the Rocky Mountains by plane would be to see them in one kind of context, as pretty scenery. But to arrive after days of hard travel across the prairies would be to see them in another way, as a goal, a promised land. If John and I and Chris arrived with this feeling and Sylvia arrived seeing them as 'nice' and 'pretty', there would be more disharmony among us than we would get from the heat and monotony of the Dakotas. Anyway I like to talk to her and I'm thinking of myself too.

In my mind, when I look at these fields, I say to her, 'See? . . . See?' and I think she does. I hope later she will see and feel a thing about these prairies I have given up talking to others about; a thing that exists here because other things are absent. She seems so depressed sometimes by the monotony and boredom of her city life, I thought maybe in this endless grass and wind she would see a thing that sometimes comes when monotony and boredom are accepted. It's here, but I have no names for it.

Now on the horizon I see something else I don't think the others see. Far off to the south-west – you can see it only from the top of this hill – the sky has a dark edge. Storm coming. That may be what has been bothering me. Deliberately shutting it out of mind, but knowing all along that with this humidity and wind it was more than likely. It's too bad, on the first day, but as I said before, on a cycle you're *in* the scene, not just watching it, and storms are definitely part of it.

If it's just thunderheads or broken line squalls you can try to ride around them, but this one isn't. That long dark streak without any preceding cirrus clouds is a cold front. Cold fronts are violent and when they are from the south-west, they are the most violent. Often they can contain tornadoes. When they come it's best just to hole up and let them pass over. They don't last long and the cold air behind them makes good riding.

Warm fronts are the worst. They can last for days. I remember Chris and I were on a trip to Canada a few years ago, got about 130 miles and were caught in a warm front of which we had plenty of warning but which we didn't understand. The whole experience was kind of dumb and sad.

We were on a little six-and-one-half-horsepower cycle, way overloaded with luggage and way underloaded with common sense. The machine could do only about forty-five miles per hour wide open against a moderate head wind. It was no touring bike. We reached a large lake in the North Woods the first night and tented amid rainstorms that lasted all night long. I forgot to dig a trench around the tent and at about two in the morning a stream of water came in and soaked both sleeping bags. The next morning we were soggy and depressed and hadn't had much sleep, but I thought that if we just got riding the rain would let up after a while. No such luck. By ten o'clock the sky was so dark all the cars had their lights on. And then it really came down.

We were wearing the ponchos which had served as a tent the night before. Now they spread out like sails and slowed our speed to thirty miles an hour wide open. The water on the road became two inches deep. Lightning bolts came crashing down all around us. I remember a woman's face looking astonished at us from the window of a passing car, wondering what on earth we were doing on a motorcycle in this weather. I'm sure I couldn't have told her.

The cycle slowed to twenty-five, then twenty. Then it started missing, coughing and popping and spluttering until, barely moving at five or six miles an hour, we found an old run-down filling station by some cutover timberland and pulled in.

At the time, like John, I hadn't bothered to learn much about motorcycle maintenance, I remember holding my poncho over my head to keep the rain from the tank and rocking the cycle between my legs. Gas seemed to be sloshing around inside. I looked at the plugs, and looked at the points, and looked at the carburettor, and pumped the kick starter until I was exhausted.

We went into the filling station, which was also a combination beer joint and restaurant, and had a meal of burned-up steak. Then I went back out and tried it again. Chris kept asking

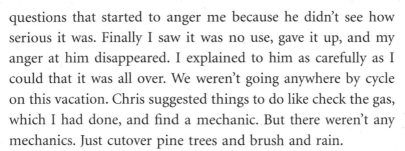

questions that started to anger me because he didn't see how serious it was. Finally I saw it was no use, gave it up, and my anger at him disappeared. I explained to him as carefully as I could that it was all over. We weren't going anywhere by cycle on this vacation. Chris suggested things to do like check the gas, which I had done, and find a mechanic. But there weren't any mechanics. Just cutover pine trees and brush and rain.

I sat in the grass with him at the shoulder of the road, defeated, staring into the trees and underbrush. I answered all of Chris's questions patiently and in time they became fewer and fewer. And then Chris finally understood that our cycle trip was over and began to cry. He was eight then, I think.

We hitchhiked back to our own city and rented a trailer and put it on our car and came up and got the cycle, and hauled it back to our own city and then started out all over again by car. But it wasn't the same. And we didn't really enjoy ourselves much.

Two weeks after the vacation was over, one evening after work, I removed the carburettor to see what was wrong but still couldn't find anything. To clean off the grease before replacing it, I turned the stopcock on the tank for a little gas. Nothing came out. The tank was out of gas. I couldn't believe it. I can still hardly believe it.

I have kicked myself mentally a hundred times for that stupidity and don't think I'll ever really, finally get over it. Evidently what I saw sloshing around was gas in the reserve tank which I had never turned on. I didn't check it carefully because I assumed the rain had caused the engine failure. I didn't understand then how foolish quick assumptions like that are. Now we are on a twenty-eight-horse machine and I take the maintenance of it very seriously.

All of a sudden John passes me, his palm down, signalling a stop. We slow down and look for a place to pull off on the gravelly shoulder. The edge of the concrete is sharp and the gravel is loose and I'm not a bit fond of this manoeuvre.

Chris asks, 'What are we stopping for?'

'I think we missed our turn back there,' John says.

I look back and see nothing. 'I didn't see any sign,' I say.

John shakes his head. 'Big as a barn door.'

'Really?'

He and Sylvia both nod.

He leans over, studies my map and points to where the turn was and then to a freeway overpass beyond it. 'We've already crossed this freeway,' he says. I see he is right. Embarrassing. 'Go back or go ahead?' I ask.

He thinks about it. 'Well, I guess there's really no reason to go back. All right. Let's just go ahead. We'll get there one way or another.'

And now tagging along behind them I think, Why should I do a thing like that? I hardly noticed the freeway. And just now I forgot to tell them about the storm. Things are getting a little unsettling.

The storm cloud bank is larger now but it is not moving in as fast as I thought it would. That's not so good. When they come in fast they leave fast. When they come in slow like this you can get stuck for quite a time.

I remove a glove with my teeth, reach down and feel the aluminium side cover of the engine. The temperature is fine. Too warm to leave my hand there, not so hot I get a burn. Nothing wrong there.

On an air-cooled engine like this, extreme over-heating can cause a 'seizure.' This machine has had one . . . in fact, three of them. I check it from time to time the same way I would check a patient who has had a heart attack, even though it seems cured.

In a seizure, the pistons expand from too much heat, become too big for the walls of the cylinders, seize them, melt to them sometimes, and lock the engine and rear wheel and start the whole cycle into a skid. The first time this one seized, my head was pitched over the front wheel and my passenger was almost on top of me. At about thirty it freed up again and started to run but I pulled off the road and stopped to see what was wrong. All my passenger could think to say was 'What did you do *that* for?'

I shrugged and was as puzzled as he was, and stood there with the cars whizzing by, just staring. The engine was so hot the air around it shimmered and we could feel the heat radiate. When I put a wet finger on it, it sizzled like a hot iron and we rode home, slowly, with a new sound, a slap that meant that the pistons no longer fit and an overhaul was needed.

I took this machine into a shop because I thought it wasn't important enough to justify getting into myself, having to learn all the complicated details and maybe having to order parts and special tools and that time-dragging stuff when I could get someone else to do it in less time — sort of John's attitude.

The shop was a different scene from the ones I remembered. The mechanics, who had once all seemed like ancient veterans, now looked like children. A radio was going full blast and they were clowning around and talking and seemed not to notice me. When one of them finally came over he barely listened to the piston slap before saying, 'Oh yeah. Tappets.'

Tappets? I should have known then what was coming.

Two weeks later I paid their bill for 140 dollars, rode the cycle carefully at varying low speeds to wear it in and then after one thousand miles opened it up. At about seventy-five it seized again and freed at thirty, the same as before. When I brought it back they accused me of not breaking it in properly, but after much argument agreed to look into it. They overhauled it again and this time took it out themselves for a high-speed road test.

It seized on *them* this time.

After the third overhaul two months later they replaced the cylinders, put in oversize carburettor jets, retarded the timing to make it run as coolly as possible and told me, 'Don't run it fast.'

It was covered in grease and did not start. I found the plugs were disconnected, connected them and started it, and now there really *was* a tappet noise. They hadn't adjusted them. I pointed this out and the kid came with an open-end adjustable wrench, set wrong, and swiftly rounded both of the sheet-aluminum tappet covers, ruining both of them.

'I hope we've got some more of those in stock,' he said.

I nodded.

He brought out a hammer and cold chisel and started to pound them loose. The chisel punched through the aluminum cover and I could see he was pounding the chisel right into the engine head. On the next blow he missed the chisel completely and struck the head with the hammer, breaking off a portion of two of the cooling fins.

'Just stop,' I said politely, feeling this was a bad dream. 'Just give me some new covers and I'll take it the way it is.'

I got out of there as fast as possible, noisy tappets, shot tappet covers, greasy machine, down the road, and then felt the vibration at speeds over twenty. At the curb I discovered two of the four engine-mounting bolts were missing and a nut was missing from the third. The whole engine was hanging on by only one bolt. The overhead-cam chain-tensioner bolt was also missing,

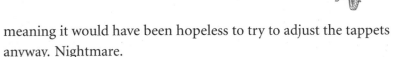

meaning it would have been hopeless to try to adjust the tappets anyway. Nightmare.

The thought of John putting his BMW into the hands of one of those people is something I have never brought up with him. Maybe I should.

I found the cause of the seizures a few weeks later, waiting to happen again. It was a little twenty-five-cent pin in the internal oil-delivery system that had been sheared and was preventing oil from reaching the head at high speeds.

The question *why* comes back again and again and has become a major reason for wanting to deliver this Chautauqua. Why did they butcher it so? These were not people running away from technology, like John and Sylvia. These were the technologists themselves. They sat down to do a job and they performed it like chimpanzees. Nothing personal in it. There was no obvious reason for it. And I tried to think back into that shop, that nightmare place, to try to remember anything that could have been the cause.

The radio was a clue. You can't really think hard about what you're doing and listen to the radio at the same time. Maybe they didn't see their job as having anything to do with hard thought, just wrench twiddling. If you can twiddle wrenches when listening to the radio that's more enjoyable.

Their speed was another clue. They were really slopping things around in a hurry and not looking where they slopped them. More money that way – if you don't stop to think that it usually takes longer or comes out worse.

But the biggest clue seemed to be their expressions. They were hard to explain. Good-natured, friendly, easygoing – and uninvolved. They were like spectators. You had the feeling they had just wandered in there themselves and somebody had handed them a wrench. There was no identification with the job. No saying, 'I am a mechanic.' At 5 PM or whenever their eight hours were in, you knew they would cut it off and not have another thought about their work. They were already trying not to have any thoughts about their work *on* the job. In their own way they were achieving the same thing John and Sylvia were, living with technology without really having to do with it. Or rather, they had something to do with it, but their own selves were outside of it, detached, removed. They were involved in it but not in such a way as to care.

Not only did these mechanics not find that sheared pin, but it was clearly a mechanic who had sheared it in the first place, by assembling the side cover plate improperly. I remembered the previous owner had said a mechanic had told him the plate was hard to get on. That was why. The shop manual had warned about this, but like the others he was probably in too much of a hurry or he didn't care.

While at work I was thinking about this same lack of care in the digital computer manuals I was editing. Writing and editing technical manuals is what I do for a living the other eleven months of the year and I knew they were full of errors, ambiguities, omissions and information so completely screwed up you had to read them six times to make any sense out of them. But what struck me for the first time was the agreement of these manuals with the spectator attitude I had seen in the shop. These were spectator manuals. It was built into the format of them. Implicit in every line is the idea that 'Here is the machine, isolated in time and in space from everything in the universe. It has no relationship to you, you have no relationship to it, other than to turn certain switches, maintain voltage levels, check for error conditions . . .' and so on. That's it. The mechanics in their

attitude toward the machine were really taking no different attitude from the manual's toward the machine, or from the attitude
I had when I brought it in there. We were all spectators. And it
occurred to me there *is* no manual that deals with the *real*
business of motorcycle maintenance, the most important aspect
of all. Caring about what you are doing is considered either
unimportant or taken for granted.

On this trip I think we should notice it, explore it a little, to
see if in that strange separation of what man is from what man
does we may have some clues as to what the hell has gone wrong
in this twentieth century. I don't want to hurry it. That itself is
a poisonous twentieth-century attitude. When you want to hurry
something, that means you no longer care about it and want to
get on to other things. I just want to get at it slowly, but carefully and thoroughly, with the same attitude I remember was
present just before I found that sheared pin. It was the attitude
that found it, nothing else.

I suddenly notice the land has flattened into a Euclidian plane.
Not a hill, not a bump anywhere. This means we have entered
the Red River Valley. We will soon be in the Dakotas.

JIM PERRIN

Extract from

TRAVELS WITH A HARLEY

Jim Perrin was born in Manchester in 1947. He is an eminent rock-climber and respected travel writer who contributes regular articles to the *Guardian, Daily Telegraph, Climber* and *TGO*. His biography of one of the greatest characters in British mountaineering, Don Whillans, *The Villain* (Hutchinson, 2005), received high praise from reviewers and was the joint winner of the 2005 Boardman Tasker Prize and also winner of the Mountain History Award at the 2005 Banff Mountain Festival.

The leafy boulevards of Boise are hard to leave behind. Two days of easy riding through the high deserts of Nevada and Oregon had brought me here. I'd had a balmy long evening on the town with Georgia Smith, who had a lop-sided grin, a good-humoured drawl, and the kind of insouciant intelligence that opens up a cavity in your chest, reaches in and gives your heart an inconsolable squeeze. She'd picked me up from J.J. Shaw's Bed & Breakfast Hotel on West Franklin in a seventies-vintage compact American car called a Skylark that was only marginally smaller than a London bus. We'd driven out to a bright terrace restaurant on a tree-lined avenue. Georgia had a Hog of her own. It was in pieces for the winter. She'd put it together again in the spring, she told me, looking up from her pudding, maple syrup trickling from her spoon. And then she weighed in: 'You gotta be crazy! Those passes, Galena Summit, The Teton – this late, on two wheels? We bin talkin' about your trip. When you get up into the Dakotas, into Montana – man, that's cold country. You better get lucky with the weather.' With that, she set out on her own reverie: drifting in canoes down rivers, traversing wilderness, wandering among mountains, sleeping out in the woods, wolf-watching, ski-ing, catching trout for breakfast. That, she told me, was hers and Idaho's vision of the American Way of Life. I was getting to like this state more and more, and that's no good when you have to be moving on.

You get susceptible on the road. 'The moral?' explained Godard, 'It's the travelling'. Idaho made me long for some immorality, or at least a few days' stasis. And the journey was scarcely begun.

I lingered over breakfast at J.J. Shaw's. Bed & Breakfast Hotels in America are not like their British counterparts. They have a cosy, laced opulence that cossets you. The other guests were doctors, washing down 20 oz. T-bones and half-a-dozen eggs with a gallon of hyper-caffeine and discussing their health insurance. I guess they needed it. I was being entertained by Ruthie White, the owner. She told me ghost stories, family histories of wilful women and ill-advised marriages – all stuff to feed the imagination of a lonely rider on the high passes. Ruthie waved me off from her porch for what I took to be a short day's ride along the Ponderosa Pine and Sawtooth Scenic Byways to Sun Valley. It was only 200 miles. I'd barely glanced at the small print on the map that spelt out 'may be closed in winter', hardly noticed the elevations. Georgia had known better. 'Get yourself some coffee in Idaho City before you hit the big time', she'd advised. 'You'll need it.' The Hog was thirsty too, so the first diner and gas station out of Boise I took her advice.

There was a feeling on me like I'd just been cast out of paradise: 'From dawn to dusk he fell,/From dusk to dewy eve', and it was still only mid-morning. I took my coffee across to a table by the window, looking down into the canyon that was taking us away from the Snake River basin. On the other side, across a continuous line of black columnar cliffs, clouds were scudding past like wreaths of smoke. The waitress came over to refill my cup. 'Those ain't Idaho plates, are they?' she ventured with a glance at The Hog, her inflection half a degree off accusation. I shook my head. 'My husband's a wildlife biologist', she continued, to explain her perspicacity or maybe just to give her view on out-of-staters, 'but my Pa, he's a rancher,' she concluded with emphasis.

'You've got conflict there, then', I suggested.

'You are so right, honey, you are just so right. Those two guys, they fight and fight and I don't ever get to hear the last of it, 'cos I'm right in the middle. Take wolves. You know we got plenty wolves here in Idaho with the new ones the gov'ment people brought in. Now my Pa, he cain't stand them, says they're nothin' but vermin an' ever' last one of them should be shot. And then my old man, he's forever tellin' me how cute they are, and sociable. I ain't never seen none of them, so who am I to believe? That's how it is when you're around guys – nothin' but contradictions!'

She gave me a dazzling, inclusive smile and retreated behind her counter. It wasn't that I felt unwelcome. It just seemed like time to leave. When I started up The Hog, even her lazy good nature was tinged with testiness and hesitance. She coughed and hiccuped and with a few explosive detonations from her exhaust as comment on all diners in cold places, thrummed on towards Moore's Summit – at 6,110 feet our first and lowest pass of the day.

You might think that one motorcycle is much like another and they are all equally soulless, dangerous, thrilling. I'm not so sure. A biker would tell you that the motorcycle is the nearest humanity has come to imbuing an artefact with character and soul. A car is simply an envelope in which you are posted more or less efficiently from one place to another (albeit with the usual vagaries attendant on the mail services). With a motorcycle, the biker would argue, you attempt to harmonise, establish some sense of balance and rhythm, even mutual understanding. At this point I want to make clear just how apposite is that terse epithet bestowed upon every two-wheeled product of the Harley-Davidson factory in Milwaukee. A Hog is a Hog is a Hog. In certain situations – on a die-straight desert highway for example, or posing at an agricultural show or stationary at a gas pump, which is its version of the feeding trough – it is perfectly capable of behaving itself and concentrating on the matter in hand. But show a 1340cc Electra-Glide Classic full-dresser in glitter-fleck metallic crimson 200 miles of narrow, twisting mountain road with a loose surface, roadworks, instant-180-degree hairpins, radical gradients, ruts and gullies and it transforms into some jittery, darting, groaning monstrous thing with which you wrestle and fight, and the harmonies of those desert highways on which your relationship was founded become a distant dream. Across Banner Summit, through Stanley and Obsidian and over the Galena Summit at 8,701 feet we were travelling through land-scape as sublime as any I'd ever seen. The Sawtooth range gnawed at the sky and I thought I'd never glimpsed more mountainy mountains. The White Cloud Peaks floated away to the east; the Salmon River prattled down through Redfish Lake; the back country beyond, ridge upon forest ridge of it, went by intriguing names like the Gospel Hump and Frank Church River of No Return Wildernesses. Lewis and Clark had threaded their way through the region somewhere over there in their epic 1804–5 crossing of America, and from the Sawtooth Scenic Byway you could be vouchsafed an insight into how wild this country is, and how recent has been its exploration and recreational exploitation.

You could have been. I had to content myself with a prolonged bout of hog-wrestling as she veered this way and that, slithered on the ice at Galena Summit, shied at flurries of snow that came gusting in on a violent wind. I made it down through the woods at last to Sun Valley, the American West's glitziest ski resort. The Hog slumped on to her stand in the portico of the Lodge and I sprawled from the saddle, cold as only a biker can know cold. In the vernacular, I was beat.

Sun Valley Lodge is exclusive. It's American neo-classical at its most expansively confident, built in the 1930's by some media multi-billionaire. All the stars, from Mary Pickford to Robert Redford, from the Kennedys to Gary Cooper had stayed here. Ernest Hemingway shot himself just down the road in Ketchum. I was thinking that not even Michael Palin would dare make a joke out of that when I became conscious of someone staring at me. Odd, I thought. The very rich whose province this is are usually liberal in their attitude towards eccentricity. I glanced back. Or rather, I looked round and down and there was a guy of about five feet two with shoulders maybe a foot wider than that and fists like hams hanging loosely at his side:

'How d'you like the bike, son?' he growled.

At that precise moment I didn't like the bike at all, and the feeling was probably mutual. But this was American soil, the Stars & Stripes was flying, and I was being asked about the other great American icon. Sometimes you just get put on the spot:

'Well . . . (long pause, not for emphasis) . . . it's got character . . . the, er, saddle's very comfortable, I like the riding position, and the way the sound system volume turns up when you twist the throttle's . . . amusing. And I love the exhaust note . . .'

'Yeah, yeah – offset crank – atmosphere at the expense of performance . . .' he responded, a little impatiently.

I'd dried up. He was watching me. 'What the hell?' I thought, and launched in:

'O.K. It's got performance half of what that engine size should offer, handles like a tank, steers like a wasp in a jam jar, push it hard on bends and neither you nor it knows where it's going, feed in the gas and it gets the message five minutes later, the gears are borrowed off a tractor . . .'

'Hold it right there!'

He held up his hand, reached in his pocket, handed me his card:

C. William Gray
Vice-President
Harley-Davidson Motor Company

'That's me, and you and I are having dinner together tonight to go through this thing in detail. You European riders are just so aggressive. Chill out, man. Get in the hot tub. See ya later.'

Extracting a foot from my mouth, I hobbled away at his command.

MATTHEW CRAWFORD

Extract from

THE CASE FOR WORKING WITH YOUR HANDS or WHY OFFICE WORK IS BAD FOR US AND FIXING THINGS IS GOOD

Matthew Crawford combines a career as a philosopher and fellow at the Institute of Advanced Studies in Culture at the University of Virginia with being a mechanic in his own motorcycle repair shop, Shockoe Moto. His thoughtful and inspirational book, *The Case for Working with Your Hands or Why Office Work is Bad for Us and Fixing Things Feels Good* (2009), is a study of how we view work today and was called a 'beautiful little book about human excellence' by the *New York Times*.

When I first started working in the bike shop, after quitting the think tank, I would come home from work and my wife would sniff at me. She'd say 'carbs' or 'brakes' as she learned to identify the various solvents used in cleaning different parts of a motorcycle. Leaving a sensible trace, my workday was at least imaginable to her. But while the filth and odours were apparent, the amount of head scratching I'd done since breakfast was not. Mike Rose writes that in the practice of surgery 'dichotomies such as concrete versus abstract and technique versus reflection break down in practice. The surgeon's judgment is simultaneously technical and deliberative, and that mix is the source of its power.' This could be said of any manual skill that is diagnostic, including motorcycle repair. You come up with an imagined train of causes for manifest symptoms and judge their likelihood before tearing anything down. This imagining relies on a stock mental library, not of natural kinds or structures, like that of the surgeon, but rather the functional kinds of an internal combustion engine, their various interpretations by different manufacturers, and their proclivities for failure. You also develop a library of sounds and smells and feels. For example, the backfire of a too-lean fuel mixture is subtly different from an ignition backfire. If the motorcycle is thirty years old, from an obscure maker that went out of business twenty years ago, its proclivities are known mostly through lore. It would probably be impossible to do such work in isolation, without access to a collective historical memory: you have to be embedded in a community of mechanic-antiquarians. These relationships are maintained by telephone, in a network of reciprocal favours that spans the country. My reliable source, Fred Cousins in Chicago, has such an encyclopedic knowledge of obscure European motorcycles that all I can offer him in exchange is regular deliveries of obscure European beer.

There is always a risk of introducing new complications when working on decrepit machines (kind of like gerontology, I suppose), and this enters the diagnostic logic. Measured in the likelihood of screw ups, the cost is not identical for all avenues of inquiry when deciding which hypothesis to pursue – for example, when trying to figure out why a bike won't start. The fasteners holding the engine cover on 1970s-era Honda are Phillips head, and they are usually rounded out and corroded. Do you *really* want to check the condition of the starter clutch, if each of the eight screws will need to be drilled out and extracted, risking damage to the engine case? Such impediments can cloud your thinking. Put more neutrally, the attractiveness of any hypothesis is determined in part by physical circumstances that have no logical connection to the diagnostic problem at hand, but a strong pragmatic bearing on it (kind of like origami). The factory service manuals tell you to be systematic in eliminating variables, but they never take into account the risks of working on old machines. So you have to develop your own decision tree for the particular circumstances. The problem is that at each node of this new tree, your own quantifiable risk aversion introduces ambiguity. There comes a point where you have to step back and get a larger gestalt. Have a cigarette and walk around the lift. Any mechanic will tell you that it is invaluable to have other mechanics around to test your reasoning against, especially if they have a different intellectual disposition.

My shop mate in the early years, Thomas Van Auken, was also an accomplished visual artist and I was repeatedly struck by his ability to literally *see* things that escaped me. I had the conceit of being an empiricist, but seeing things is not always a simple matter. Even on the relatively primitive vintage bikes that were our speciality, some diagnostic situations contain so many variables, and symptoms can be so under-determining of causes, that explicit analytical reasoning comes up short. What is required then is the kind of judgment that arises only from experience; hunches rather than rules. I quickly realized there was more thinking going on in the bike shop than in my previous job at the think tank.

Socially, being the proprietor of a bike shop in a small city gives me a feeling I never had before. I feel I have a place in society. Whereas 'think tank' is an answer that, at best, buys you a few seconds when someone asks what you do and you try to figure out what it is that you in fact do, with 'motorcycle mechanic' I get immediate recognition. I barter services with machinists and metal fabricators, which has a very different feel than transactions with money, and further increases my sense of belonging to a community. There are three restaurants in Richmond with cooks whose bikes I have restored, where unless I deceive myself I am treated as a sage benefactor. I feel pride before my wife when we go out to dinner and are given preferential treatment, or simply a hearty greeting. There are group rides, and there used to be bike night every Tuesday at a certain bar. Sometimes one or two people would be wearing my shop's t-shirt, which felt good.

DAN WALSH

Extract from

THESE ARE THE DAYS THAT MUST HAPPEN TO YOU

In 2000 cult motorcycle journalist Dan Walsh departed London on a Yamaha XT Desert Rat headed for Africa, travelling from Dakar to Ghana to South Africa. He then went on to North and South America with his BMW F650GS Dakar.

Rebel, vagabond, poet, biking drifter, Dan's column in *Bike* magazine was an addictive, lyrical, volatile, deranged and awesome exhibition of writing from the edge. Take his description of Chile:

'For me, Chile will always be South America's supermodel sister – very beautiful but too long, too skinny, and too expensive to ride, and despite the groovy exterior, unpleasantly right-wing underneath.'

Many entries from this addictive column were brought together in the explosive and, as the jacket blurb says, 'coruscatingly funny' collection, *These Are the Days that Must Happen to You* (Century 2008).

I love my bike. 'I love your bike too much,' snorted Buffalo the soldier, giving me a punch that might have been considered matey if it hadn't been for the AK swinging from his bowling ball-muscled arms. 'In Accra, it is under my protection. If I see anyone else riding it, I will shoot them dead.' Which was reassuring only as long as he remembered my face. And transformed my XT into the vehicle for the perfect crime. Enter stage left the mockney shyster who's been trying to sleep with my girl while I've been away. 'Hi. Dan. Nice bike.' 'Hi, Mac. Sure is. Tell you what, why not take it for a spin – I know a great route across the cliffs past the barracks.' Praise the Lord and pass the ammunition.

I hated my bike. 'You're going round the world on that?' sniggered girlfriend Lou. 'But it's a kid's bike!' And my wagging tail drooped dish-rag. Limp. Forget power-to-weight ratios, to hell with race-track geometry, I want a bike that makes me sexy. The only time it ever looked sexy was with Lou on board, all tippy-toes cowboy boots and too-tight Levi's, zipping up and down the beach in Senegal. 'Gosh, you must be a real woman to handle a beast like that. Fancy some taboo sex?' Not sexy, just slow. Changing down to maintain an asthmatic uphill 60 mph was something I hoped I'd left behind years ago when I jumped off the CG125 into the brave new world of a CX. But the further south I got, the more versatility overtook top speed. And by the time I'd reached Tangier and effortlessly bounded up a set of steps into the hotel courtyard, I knew I was riding a winner. Last time I tried the same manoeuvre was on a ZX9 – it took three men, an hour and some particularly filthy cursing. Can't be that slow if it gained me an extra hour in Africa's sleaziest bar.

I crash my bike. 'I can't believe I've made it all the way across the Sahara without throwing it away' was all the subvocal encouragement that the God of Counted Chickens (the most malicious of deities) needed to kick away my front wheel and scud me into a sandbank. Crashing on tarmac is shocking – skid, gasp, slam, followed by nervous body and bike damage report. But crashing off-road is just silly clowning – yelp, tumble, dead-cat bounce, pick yourself up and do it all over again. More than crashing, I like dropping my bike. Side stand on wet sand is a recent favourite. Always seem to look up just in time to see it swaying like a waddling toddler before, whoops-a-daisy!, it flops onto its cushioning saddlebag nappies. Last year a couple of clumsy scallies knocked over a Busa I'd borrowed. The invoice touched two grand. Eight comedy drops later, and the only damage to the XT is a banana'd clutch. Perfect for overlanding monkeys.

I fix my bike. 'Punctures will be your most common problem,' warned wise overlander Chris Scott. Most common and least dignified. Last time was in Burkina Faso – strutting into a dusty village, imperiously waving a cheery 'Bonjour!' when the front went bang!, and I veered into a ditch. Big crowd, but no mechanics – so it was up to me to get the spoons out and dive in. And, dayum, after thirty years of paying a buck to pass the buck, it felt good. Me, the bike and no intermediary, a proper bloke doing proper blokes' work. The fact that I had to take the tyre off three bastard times 'cause I couldn't get the patch to stick and then holed the tube with the levers barely ruffled my new-found Zen-like serenity.

I trust my bike. 'Start, you vicious, vicious bastard' is a quote from Rupert Paul that pops up every time I unfaithfully think maybe the trip would have been groovier on a Husqvarna or WR400, and I picture that hard man of publishing sweating like a sieve on a chilly day in Cheshire, pumping away at the recalcitrant Husky. What with border guards, dunes, bandits and my own riding handicaps, the last thing I need is to worry whether the bike will start. Glad as I am that Yamaha went to such trouble to fix the kicker, I've only ever used it in London as a pose. I'll save my kicking for something that deserves it.

I even talk to my bike. 'Come on, little *hmar*, don't fail me now!' was the superstitious battle cry that led Germans and Tuaregs alike to turn away, slightly embarrassed, tapping the sides of their heads. Divvy as it sounds, it's even got a name – the Yamahmar, 'hmar' being the Arabic word for donkey. The parallels are obvious – both much-maligned beasts of burden, overloaded and abused by cruel owners. And I like donkeys 'cause they invariably wink when I say hello.

Yep, I love my bike. Which is good, because it's all I've got left. 'Dear John,' said Lou as she made a laughing-stock April Fool of me. Home no longer exists. So I'm packing my bags again, and hitting the road again, whistling 'Hey Joe' while pushing hard for motorcycle emptiness.

Keep drifting? I've got no fucking choice.

MAT OXLEY

Extract from

STEALING SPEED

Mat Oxley is a widely published motorcycling journalist, commentator, author and ex-motorcycle racer. *Stealing Speed* (2009) tells the extraordinary story of the technological development of the two-stroke engine by Walter Kaaden of the East German MZ company utilising the experience and ideas he gained in World War II during his work on the V2 programme based at Peenemünde. The dominance of these engines became the subject of a le Carré-esque Cold War plot when Kaaden's star rider, Ernst Degner, betrayed his friend and mentor and defected, selling the plans and his own riding and mechanical expertise to the Japanese manufacturer, Suzuki.

This extract relates Degner's victory on the Suzuki at the Isle of Man TT and calls on Oxley's own experience as a TT winner and lap record holder to describe the sensation of riding arguably the most exciting, demanding and dangerous laps in motorsport.

Degner was dimly aware of a loud banging noise; his head swirled into consciousness. In the gloomy first light of dawn the room seemed unfamiliar. More banging. 'Ernst, it is time to get up, time to get up.' Degner fumbled for his rather smart wristwatch lying on the bedside table and squinted at the dial. It said 4.15am.

He dressed quickly, took his leathers, boots, gloves and pudding-basin helmet from the wardrobe and made his way downstairs, still a bit wobbly on his feet. Twenty minutes later he was at the Glencrutchery Road start line in full riding gear while a bleary-eyed, overalled Suzuki mechanic warmed up his RM62 for early morning practice. The pair stood in the midst of a few dozen riders and mechanics, all of them shrouded from the outside world by a warm, sickly fog of two-stroke fumes. No jokes, no banter, just looks of quiet concentration from the mechanics and 1,000 yard stares from the riders, all of them keeping their hopes and their fears to themselves in the cool, grey dawn. Degner fiddled with his goggles, focusing his nervous energy into carefully applying demister, one drop of Fairy Liquid on each lens.

Not all the machines were smoky two-strokes. Off to the left by the paddock gate a rider sat across his AJS 250 single while a mechanic steadied a primus stove beneath the crankcases, warming the engine oil before firing the machine into life.

Through the gate marched an ordered line of three uniformed Honda mechanics, each pushing a Honda RC111, the jewel-like 17,000rpm four-stroke that Suzuki had to beat.

Twenty yards further up the Glencrutchery Road stood a stout, middle-aged lady in a headscarf holding a blackboard. Scrawled across the board in chalky, barely legible handwriting were the words:

'morning practice
riders beware
rain in Ramsey
fog on the mountain
Black Hut to Brandywell'

The Isle of Man TT was the biggest motorcycle race in the world, where manufacturers could make or break reputations. The event had always been notoriously tough, ever since the inaugural races in 1907 that had been designed to test touring machines to the very limit, hence 'Tourist Trophy'. Even in the late 1950s and early 1960s it was only the bike-racing event that mattered throughout the globe. To the nascent Japanese motorcycle industry the TT meant everything. In Japan very little was known about other grand prix events, hence Soichiro Honda's proud pledge in 1954, five years before his motorcycles became the first Japanese machines to race in Europe: 'I here avow my definite intention that I will participate in the TT races and I proclaim with my fellow employees that I will pour in all my energy and creative powers to win.'

Honda-san, and later Mr Suzuki and others, knew full well that Norton, Triumph, MV Agusta and a dozen other factories had built their brand image at the TT, making millions by testing their engineering prowess against the gruelling Manx roads, proving that their machinery was both rapid and rugged. It was motorcycling's ultimate exercise in corporate PR.

And yet the event had the genteel air of an English village fête about it, with the discordant twist of death and destruction lurking in the shadows. The TT was run by old boys in blazers and enthusiastic ladies who might otherwise have invested their energies in the Women's Institute, They talked about the Island's capricious weather like they were getting ready for a spot of gardening, apparently unaware that fog and rain usually meant more accidents, more broken legs, more fatalities. Tradition mattered on the Island, so practice went ahead whatever the conditions. As the chaps in blazers would say: 'No such thing as inclement weather, old boy, only inappropriate clothing.'

Degner did not like early morning practice, whatever the weather, and not only because he thought it wasn't right that he was required to take risks with his own life before breakfast. Less importantly but more crucially, the cold, dewy air played havoc with carburettor settings, so whatever main jet worked at dawn probably wouldn't be right for the race, scheduled for 11.00am on the last day of race week. But he needed every practice lap he could get and this was his final chance to test the RM62 over the Mountain circuit.

Suzuki teammate Mitsui Itoh had been fastest in the first session at the start of practice week, just two seconds faster than Degner over the 37¾-mile lap. In the second practice outing Luigi Taveri was quickest. Honda weren't planning on getting beaten. The RC 111s had started the season with six-speed gearboxes and been badly defeated. A month later at the French Grand Prix they had used eight-speed gearboxes and still been vanquished. Three weeks later, halfway through TT practice week, a crate arrived in Douglas from Japan – packed with brand-new ten-speed gearboxes.

Degner had been busy all week, calculating the correct jetting and fine-tuning the gearing to extract every last tenth of a horsepower out of the little RM engine. And it worked. In Saturday's final practice session he was more than a minute ahead of Itoh, and Taveri was a further few seconds down in third place. He returned to the Fernleigh hotel for breakfast, happy in the knowledge that all he had to do now was extrapolate his carburettor settings for the 11.00am start the following Friday. He was ready to race.

Degner knew how to ride fast at the TT. The Island roads were no more than country lanes, but they weren't all hairpin bends and corkscrew corners; much of the course was ultra-fast, often flat-out in top gear mile after mile, even on bigger, faster motorcycles. It was through these sections that TTs were won and lost. The really quick corners were where the most time could be gained, especially through the fastest stretches of road where a few mph gained through one corner would be carried through the next two or three miles of flat-in-top, under-the-bubble riding. Of course, these really fast corners were also the most dangerous. It made grim logic: the bigger the risk, the bigger the reward.

Thus the secret to TT speed was economy in riding style and maintaining momentum, sweeping through the corners as smooth and fast as possible – no panicky last-moment grab for the brakes to scrub off speed, hoping the tyres would keep gripping all the way to the apex. If you knew what was good for you, you took it nice and smooth with a nice, late entry into each corner for a nice, late apex. That way you had less chance of running wide on the exit and into a dry-stone wall. Degner didn't want to become a part of the Manx scenery.

There are more than 250 corners to a TT lap, and they all needed memorising. Forgetting where you were or mistaking one corner for another was an easy but potentially lethal mistake. And your first mistake might be your last. No room for error – literally.

Riders needed to know everything about every corner on the course; they needed to know what state the tarmac was in, where the bumps were, where the manhole covers were, where the road switched from positive camber to negative camber or vice-versa, where sections of road stayed wet for longer after a rain shower and which bits of tarmac melted on hot, sunny days. All this information needed to be learned and logged.

And then riders had to learn the braking points for every corner, how many gears to change down into each corner and, most important of all, which line to take through each corner. Sometimes the line was a straightforward racing arc; as close as you dared to the stone wall on the outside of the corner, swooping across the road towards the bus stop on the inside, then as close as you dared to the telegraph pole on the way out. The faster you went, the more road you used, so if you wanted to win you needed to miss the scenery by inches, not feet. Riders knew they had found the fastest line, the ultimate trajectory when they returned to the paddock with scrape marks on their helmets and scuffs on their leathers. Heart racing, blood pumping, they had just been closer to death and thus more alive than they had ever been.

Most cornering lines weren't just straightforward arcs; most were complicated by bumps, camber changes and dodgy patches of tarmac. Riders needed to know where to hold on tight and wrestle like hell, and where to relax and let the motorcycle find its own way. And sometimes what looked like the right line on the way in certainly wasn't the right line on the way out. Get it right and you were quick. Get it wrong and you were either slow or dead.

Then there was the machine to consider. How was the gearing? How was the jetting? Was it too rich up the mountain or too lean near the coast? Might it be worth adjusting the jetting or changing the gearing to sacrifice performance through one part of the course for better performance through another more crucial section?

Degner would drift off to sleep each night riding the 37¾ miles in his mind – visualising every corner, ever gear shift, every telegraph pole, remembering the little tricks that might keep him alive or, even better, help him win the race.

Finally the time had come: 11.00am, Friday 8 June 1962 and Degner was pushing off from the start line, watched by a crowd of officials, dignitaries and spectators.

His mind was already applying itself to the first real challenge, the eighth-gear plunge down Bray Hill just 500 yards into the lap. He was now where he liked to be most of all: totally alone, hunkered over the fuel tank, just him and his RM62 against the world. Nothing else mattered, nothing else at all, except using all his bravery and skill to get to the finish line as quickly as possible. Loneliness was the way it was on the Island. There were no massed starts as was the norm at other grand prix events – the course was far too dangerous for that. Instead, riders were sent plummeting down the Glencrutchery Road in pairs at ten-second intervals, the race result decided on corrected time.

Except this time Degner started all alone. He had been due to start alongside Tom Phillis at the very front of the pack, but Phillis wasn't there. Twenty-four hours earlier he had been cremated in Douglas cemetery, next to the start line. The man who had beaten Degner to the 1961 125 world championship had been killed two days earlier during the Junior race. The Australian was one of two riders who died that afternoon. At the end of the week the national dailies christened the Isle of Man 'Bloodbath Island'.

Of the survivors, Degner knew who his main rivals would be: definitely Taveri, who was starting 30 seconds behind; maybe Tommy Robb on another factory-entered Honda, starting 40 seconds back; possibly his own team-mate Mitsuo Itoh, starting 50 seconds back. He would be kept informed of his position relevant to his rivals by Suzuki pit signallers at three points around the course: at the end of the Sulby straight (where they could communicate with the pits by telephoning from a local's house), coming out of Ramsey at Waterworks, and at the pits. The signallers noted down the latest times broadcast over the circuit PA system, then passed on the information via blackboards.

When he raced past the pits at the end of the first lap his board told him that he had a 15 second lead on Taveri, who was neck and neck with Robb. Much of the first few miles of the lap the RM was flat-out in eighth gear. Degner's engine geared perfectly, carburating beautifully, crisp in mid-range, sharp at the top end, happily singing to 10,900 rpm. But would it last? As he braked into the sharp right-hander by the Ballacraine Hotel, eight miles into the second and last lap, he knew he was entering the darkest, deadliest phase of the race.

For the next few miles the course followed the west bank of the river Neb, the narrow road threading busily left and right. Through Dorans Bend and Laurel Bank the road was more like a tunnel, shrouded in semi-darkness by heavy trees, a thousand shades of summer greens, and hemmed in by steep rock faces and dry-stone walls. 'If you crashed there,' says Tommy Robb, 'you were too soft to take it.'

That day he treated the Laurel Bank section with even more respect than usual, for it was here two days earlier that poor old Tom had bought it. Phillis had been chasing Gary Hocking and Mike Hailwood. He had overcooked it at the right-hander immediately prior to Laurel Bank, slamming into the rock face. An ambulance rushed Phillis down the back roads to Ballacraine where doctors pronounced him dead. Phillis's wife Betty, his daughter Brenda Ann, aged two, his son Thomas Braddan, who had been born during TT week the previous year, were all on the Island to watch the races.

Two miles later Degner was climbing steeply up and out into the open again, Snaefell Mountain looming above his right shoulder. To his left the Irish Sea twinkled in the midday sun of a perfect English summer's day. Cresting the top of Creg Willey's Hill he shifted into sixth gear at precisely 10,900rpm, just before the power began to fade, then repeated the procedure into seventh and eighth gears. It was a well-rehearsed operation, the RM62 required several hundred gear changes each TT lap.

Once he was in top gear his attention returned to contorting his body into its least wind-resistant form. Aerodynamics mattered in 50cc racing even more than they did in 125s, and nowhere more than at the TT. The RM62 had been designed to allow its rider to assume his most aerodynamic form, not without some discomfort. Degner's torso was flattened over the fuel tank until his spine was parallel; his head was twisted backward by seventy degrees to peer ahead. His arms were stretched forward to the handlebars that had been acutely angled to get his hands inside the fairing, now moulded in newfangled glass-fibre instead of hand-beaten in aluminium. His elbows were bent at 45 degrees and pressed in hard against the fuel tank. His knees were tucked into the back of his upper arms, just a couple of inches from his chest. It wasn't comfortable but it was fast, and Degner wasn't worried about being comfortable – only speed mattered.

Aiming right after the Cronk-y-Voddy crossroads he was heading downhill again, gaining speed, his left elbow scattering wildflowers as he swooped right and then left between the hedgerows of Drinkwaters, christened after Ben Drinkwater, who had died there in 1949. This was Island irony: a good number of TT corners are named after riders who paid the ultimate price for getting them very wrong.

Over Barregarrow top, accelerating downhill at a rate into Barregarrow bottom, swinging hard left through the 13th Milestone and bursting through the right-hander into Kirkmichael village, then riding the centre of the road all the way to Birkin's Bend. It was here that racing aristocrat Archie Birkin had lost his life during an early morning practice session for the 1927 TT. Birkin had swerved to avoid a horse and cart delivering fish to a nearby village and slammed into the road at 80mph. Only after his death did the TT organisers think to amend the Road Closing Act to close the roads to normal traffic during practice sessions.

Working his way eastwards across the north of the Island, Degner flew the little Suzuki over the humpback bridge in Ballaugh village and locked his arms against the petrol tank as he fought his way over the hellish bumps of Quarry Bends and Kerrowmoar, then back into the racing tuck for the flat-out run towards Ramsey. The crowd in Parliament Square could hear his solitary approach from a mile or two away, a hubbub of expectation went through the spectators at the distant sound, like an angry wasp. Slowly, relentlessly the buzz got louder, the pitch rising and falling through every corner, through every gear change. The crowds craned towards Schoolhouse corner to catch a glimpse.

Degner swept through Schoolhouse, barely visible behind the Suzuki's bodywork, sat up at the last moment and braked, his left foot tap dancing through the gearbox – eighth, seventh, sixth, fifth, fourth, third and finally second – for the dead-slow right-hander that took him into the square. The crowd, standing obediently behind makeshift wooden barriers, visibly winced as the deafening zing-zing-zing of the downshifts bounced off the grey granite walls.

Accelerating out of Ramsey, Degner began the long, lonely climb towards the peak of Snaefell, adjusting the air-mixture lever on the left handlebar to lean the carburation as he gained altitude. After the Gooseneck right-hander the road opened out across bleak, windswept fells where the Suzuki's speed (though some would argue that it actually belonged to Walter Kaaden) would really tell over the chasing Hondas. Tucked in until every muscle screamed for release, eyes resolutely peering through the Perspex screen, chin chattering against the fuel tank until it bled, he rode up the Mountain Mile and through Brandywell, the highest point on the course at 1,400 feet. Then, like a roller-coaster that had rumbled to the peak of its ride and tipped over into the descent, suddenly gaining speed with a dizzying, stomach-churning rush, it was downhill all the way to the finish line in Douglas six miles away. The engine sang more eagerly than ever with gravity on its side, Degner allowing the revs to creep towards 11,500rpm as he hurriedly thumbed the air lever to richen the mixture. Even so, his fingers always hovered over the clutch lever, ears straining for the faintest sign of impending mechanical doom.

His heart was in his mouth as he rushed into blind, 100mph multi-apex corners that demanded total commitment and utter accuracy. This was the part of the course he enjoyed most of all. He attacked these corners with head firmly beneath the bubble and without a thought for the consequences of getting them wrong. There were no walls on the mountain section – nothing to be scared of. This wasn't a claustrophobic rat-run like the lower reaches of the circuit. And yet any miscalculation here would be just as deadly, ejecting rider and machine into the blue yonder and down the mountainside, scattering lazily grazing sheep in all directions as metal and muscle self-destructed during the precipitous descent.

Almost before he knew it he was past the Creg-ny-Baa pub and onward and downward to the Glencrutchery road, from where he had pushed off just over an hour and 75 miles ago. Degner has beaten Taveri by a comfortable 18 seconds, Robb a further 13 seconds back. The Suzuki Motor Company had made the breakthrough, its first world championship race win after two years of humiliating failures. And not only that, they had won a race at the biggest racing event of them all, round the toughest racetrack on the planet. Suzuki had conquered motorcycling's Everest. And they'd won the team prize too, Mitsuo Itoh finishing fifth and Michio Ichino sixth – three of the little silver and blue machines in the six points-scoring places. Suzuki had proved that they could build fast motorcycles and, just as crucially, that they could build engines that would go the distance.

Degner's TT-winning average might have been a humble 75.12mph but it was still four mph faster than Suzuki's best 125 had managed two years earlier. The factory's win was doubly significant because it was also the first two-stroke TT success since 1938, when DKW had won the 250 race. At least Zschopau technology was back on top!

Obviously, there was a big party. 'After the prize-giving we went off to one of the nicest hotels in Douglas and had a bloody good shindig,' remembers Perris. 'We all got horribly sloshed – us and the Japanese. It was a lovely team.'

The British press feted Degner, praising him for his victory and for his decision to turn his back on the communists and throw in his lot with the capitalists: 'For Ernst Degner the result was the happiest pay-off to a gamble which must have required high moral and physical courage. Just the attributes, in fact, of a successful TT racer!' wrote *Motorcycle News*. No doubt Kaaden would have questioned the bit about high moral courage.

VALENTINO ROSSI

Extract from

WHAT IF I HADN'T TRIED IT

Valentino Rossi was born in Urbino, Italy in 1979, the son of Grand Prix motorcycle racer Graziano Rossi.

Rossi first emerged onto the motorcycle racing scene in 1996 when he rode 125cc machines for Aprilia. The following year he won the World Championship for Aprilia and moved up to the 250cc category with the same team and subsequently became World Champion in 1997. This phenomenal personality and technical genius went on to win the final 500cc championship with Honda in 2001 and the first MotoGP title in 2002 and 2003 with the same team. Rossi, taunted by critics who suggested that his success was down to the dominant Honda machines, duly left for the poorly performing Yamaha team and won back-to-back titles in 2004 and 2005 and once again in 2008. He now rides for the iconic Italian marque Ducati in an all-Italian dream team.

Valentino Rossi, nicknamed 'The Doctor' and always riding under the number 46, transcends the sport like few other riders have ever done, is a worldwide superstar and is, without question, the greatest motorcycle racer ever.

When we swerved to the left, bent right over, fully in third gear, at 170 kilometres per hour, from my Honda all I could see were the upper exhaust pipes of his Yamaha. He was still ahead of me, just as we came into the turn at the top of the hill, right where the horizon ends and you begin to disappear behind it. I was glued to him. It was the dying moments of an open shoot-out which began with eight riders and was now down to two. The two of us. Me and Max Biaggi.

The final reckoning of the 2001 championship. Last lap. Last tough spot. Last point of attack. Last chance . . . for me.

That turn is on a stretch of asphalt spread like butter over a shallow, green hill. It clings to the hill tightly, following every contour. It's like a long 'S', first left, then right, and the apex is the top of the hill. Before you get there, you're going uphill. After that, it's all downhill. When you go into the corner, you can't see what's on the other side. You have to ride from memory. You have no idea when you can brake, you only begin to understand when you're on the other side and if you haven't picked the right spot, it's too late, there's nothing you can do about it.

I planned an outside trajectory, so that I could be on his right in the brief downhill stretch and then on the inside on the following turn. There is only one way to get through that turn, in first gear, after downshifting from fourth.

If you are first coming out of there, it's over. You've won. I felt my elbow brush up against his Yamaha, first his exhaust pipe, then his rear tyre. I was taking a huge risk of course I was. But I had to. It was the only way to get ahead of him when it came to brake. And that's what I did. When he realised what was happening, I was right there, next to him, on the outside. And suddenly it was too late for him to react. We came down side by side, and I went into the tight right turn first, and stayed ahead in the long left turn that followed, crossing the finish line ahead of him.

And that was how I won the 2001 Australian Grand Prix and became the new 500cc World Champion.

Three years later, Sete Gibernau and I found ourselves in the exact same spot on the same track. He was expecting me to attack him, just as I had attacked Biaggi. He knew what was coming – it was the last lap and I had already tried to attack him a few turns earlier, but then I had made a crucial mistake and had allowed Gibernau to regain the lead. This time, I decided to go inside, at the entrance of the uphill turn, so that I'd be ahead just as we went downhill. I wanted to seal the victory early, before the long downhill stretch, so I went for it, just as we came into the long turn and the elevation changed.

'I did it!' I thought to myself. But my elation lasted a mere instant. It was a false dawn. Gibernau came off his brakes and closed my path, and we reached the top of the hill together, with his Honda nudging the front wheel of my Yamaha. But then, suddenly, I saw him going wide, too wide. He couldn't close the trajectory, he was blowing the turn.

'Oh, you're going wide, aren't you . . . yeah, you're going wide . . . yes, yes, you can't do it . . . you're too wide. . . I'm coming through!' The thought dashed through my mind as I hit the gas and accelerated past him.

In that part of the track, you're going very fast and you're bent right over. You can't touch your brakes and you can't get up. Once you're in, you're in. If you made the slightest mistake, if your speed isn't right, you're out.

Gibernau came into the turn too fast, while I had exactly the right speed. I passed him, going ahead into the last, slow right turn – just as I had done three years earlier.

And that was how I won the 2004 Australian Grand Prix.

I won with the Yamaha. I beat the Honda. And I retained my MotoGP world title.

Those were two glorious moves, coming as they did at the climax of two outstanding races in two intense seasons. The first in 500cc, the second in MotoGP.

I thought of the coincidences. They occurred in the exact same spot, three years apart. And I thought there was something magical about them. The 2001 and 2004 titles were not only the most hard-fought, but also the most significant among those I have won. I won them on the same track, Philip Island, making two incredible manoeuvres, in the same spot, in the same crucial moment of the season. And in each case I wanted to put the final nail in the coffin and secure the title.

That long left turn where I made two of the overtaking moves I enjoyed the most in my entire career, is probably the most exciting stretch of a fantastic track that will forever be close to my heart. At Philip Island, there is the long initial straightaway, and following that you reach the ocean after a series of turns – some wide, some tight, with changes in speed and elevation. You reach the ocean and then you leave it behind, twice, before joining a long ramp which takes you straight up to the famous long left turn. But just before that, there is a very fast chicane:

you arrive in fourth gear, at 200kph, go down to third gear and 170kph to negotiate the 'right–left' change in direction and, finally, you take on that long uphill curve. On that long turn, you spend what seems like an eternity bent over, flying along at very high speeds, unable to see what's ahead. It is one of the most beautiful, fastest and difficult turns in the whole MotoGP tour. You have to be extremely accurate and sensitive to negotiate your way through it, and it's one of those spots where the quality of the rider makes all the difference. Just as, to me, it makes all the difference if it's the last lap or not.

I love beating my opponents on the last lap. It's the most exciting way to win a race. Sure, sometimes it would probably be best to avoid problems, rush out ahead and build up a huge lead, but there are times when you realize you can't build a gap with the others, and at those times it's best if you wait for the last lap. It's the ultimate showdown. You've prepared, lap after lap. You've studied your main opponent's trajectories, the way he takes every turn; you know where he's strongest and where his weaknesses are, you know where he's vulnerable if you attack him. It's the ultimate rush. On that last lap, you may be able to surprise your opponent once, at best, but that's it. He won't fall for anything after that. Everything becomes tougher.

I think back to 2001 and 2004 and I know that Biaggi and Gibernau gave everything they had. I know, because I did the same. It was the crucial moment, the stakes were huge, it wasn't just about the world title; at stake were the future paths of our racing careers.

In 2001, Biaggi and I were competing to win what would be not just our first title in the 500cc, but also the final title ever in that category. The following season, of course, the MotoGP era kicked off, replacing the 500cc category. At the time, I had only been racing 500cc for one season and so, for me, this was my first and only chance to win the title I had always dreamed about. I had only the one chance to win it and that chance was now. Biaggi was in the exact same boat as me, but I desperately wanted to be the last ever 500cc world champion.

The stakes were very high in 2004 as well, given what happened the year before: I had left Honda and gone to Yamaha, in search of new challenges. I was determined to prove that I could win even without a bike, the Honda, which everyone thought was invincible.

I chose Yamaha, a team which was in serious difficulty, which only made the challenge that much greater. This wasn't just about winning another title, it was about resentment and pride, rancour and honour. I knew that the 2004 season could put an end to an entirely different issue and therefore there was so much more pressure. I knew that if I could win right away, with a Yamaha, in my first season, it would change the face of motor-cycling for ever. And that's what happened in Australia, on the hills of Philip Island, where I put the finishing touches on an adventure which had begun in South Africa.

Yes, South Africa. Welkom, the young city located in Orange Free State. The date was 18 April 2004, a day which will long live in the history of motorcycle racing. I won my very first race with Yamaha. It was also the very first race of the 2004 World Championship. It was something absolutely unthinkable, even for me.

You may have seen me stop at the edge of the track, getting off my beautiful Yamaha, and watched as I sat down next to her, wrapping my arms around my knees and lowering my head. You may have wondered what I was doing; perhaps you thought I was overcome with emotion and was having a quiet sob of relief. In fact, I wasn't. Not at all. Behind my black visor, I was laughing. Laughing heartily at that. In that moment, huddled next to my bike on the grass, resting against her tyres, just me and my Yamaha, I was laughing. Laughing because of the incredible feeling of pride, relief and happiness which had overcome me.

'And so in the end I was right!' I thought to myself. 'I can't believe it, I screwed them all . . . what a show!'

ROBERT HUGHES

MYTH OF THE MOTORCYCLE HOG

Robert Hughes was born in 1938 in Sydney, Australia.
He moved to London at the age of 26 and became a
journalist writing for, amongst other publications,
The Times, the *Daily Telegraph* and the *Observer*. Since
1970 he has lived and worked in the United States where
he has been art critic for *Time* magazine for thirty years.

He has been honoured by numerous institutions
and is a distinguished author of such books as *The Fatal
Shore*, *Barcelona* and *Goya*.

Has any means of transport ever suffered a worse drubbing than the motorcycle? In the 17 years since Stanley Kramer put Marlon Brando astride a Triumph in *The Wild One*, big bikes and those who ride them have been made into apocalyptic images of aggression and revolt – Greasy Rider on an iron horse with 74-cu.-in. lungs and ape hanger bars, booming down the freeway to rape John Doe's daughter behind the white clapboard bank: swastikas, burnt rubber, crab lice and filthy denim. It has long been obvious that the bike was heir to the cowboy's horse in movies; but if Trigger had been loaded with the sado-erotic symbolism that now, after dozens of exploitation flicks about Hell's Angels, clings to any Harley chopper, the poor nag could not have moved for groupies. As an object to provoke linked reactions of desire and outrage, the motorcycle has few equals – provided it is big enough.

When *Easy Rider* was released, it looked for a time as though public attitudes might soften. A lot of people were on the side of Captain America and his fringed partner Billy, shotgunned off their glittering, raked choppers on a Southern back road. But for every cinemagoer who vicariously rode with Fonda and Hopper in that movie, there were probably ten who went with their redneck killers in the pickup truck. The chorus from press and TV remains pretty well unchanged, resembling the bleat of Orwell's sheep in *Animal Farm*: 'Four wheels good, two wheels bad!' The image of the biker as delinquent will take a long time to eradicate. 'You meet the nicest people on a Honda,' proclaims the Japanese firm that has cornered nearly 50% of the bike market in the U.S.; but the general belief is that you still meet the nastiest ones on a chopper.

To the public, the names of the outlaw or semi-outlaw motorcycle clubs is a litany of imps in the pit, from the Animals, and Axemen, through the Equalizers and Exterminators, the Marauders and Mongols, the Raiders and Road Vultures, to the Warlocks and Wheels of Soul. The unsavoury names with which these gangs have christened themselves are apt to make the public forget that their collective membership is probably no more than 3,000, the merest fraction of the 3,000,000 people who regularly ride bikes in the U.S. In fact, these 'outlaws' on the road are infinitely less of a threat than the driver of a station wagon with two martinis under his seat belt.

The myth goes roaring on. Business, though, may kill it, for bikes are big business today. At the end of World War II there were fewer than 200,000 registered motorcycles in the U.S. Today there are nearly 2,500,000, most of them imports from Japan, Germany and Britain. The majority are small, almost civilized creatures, below 500cc. in engine capacity. But the popularity of the big snorting monsters, which can go from a standstill to 60 mph in less than six seconds flat and cruise comfortably on freeways at 90 mph, has also ascended. It has its perversities.

To the four-wheeled culture, there is something inexplicable about the very idea of owning such a bike. A big machine is expensive: a new Honda Four costs nearly as much as a Volkswagen; a big Harley, almost $1,000 more. Choppers, the Fabergé Easter eggs of the bike world, are even worse. When all the stripping, chroming, raking, molding, metal flaking and polishing are done, a chopper, righteously gleaming from fishtail exhaust to brakeless front wheel, may have cost its owner $5,000 in materials and labour. Insurance is heavy, since to many companies the fact of owning a bike is prima-facie evidence of irresponsibility. The risk of theft is high, especially in cities, where case-hardened steel chains and medieval-looking padlocks must tether the mount if one so much as stops for a hamburger.

Highway cops dislike bikers and are apt to assume that a Hell's Angel lurks slavering and Benzedrined inside every rider; they take a sour glee in plastering the riders with tickets for the slightest infraction. Worst of all, there are accidents. Big bikes are superb manifestations of engineering skill, but they are utterly vulnerable. There is no body shell, no padding, no safety belt – nothing to cushion the body that wrenched forward over the bars at 50 mph may be no more than a leaking bag of tissue and bone fragments when the concrete has finished with it. On any long trip, moreover, the biker stands to encounter at least one car-swaddled Milquetoast with blood in his eye whose hope is to run him off the road. Highways are the bullrings of American insecurity and every biker knows it, or ends up in a hospital.

So why ride? There are, of course, impeccable reasons. Bikes are easy to park, they save gas, they pollute the air less than cars. But the impeccable reasons are not always the real ones. Buying a bike, particularly a big motorcycle, is buying an experience that no other form of transport can give: a unique high that like pot has spun its own culture around itself. The name of the game is freedom. A biker, being more mobile, is on a different footing from a driver. The nightmares of traffic afflict him less. Instead of being trapped in a cumbersome padded box, frozen into the glacier of unmoving steel and winking red taillights on the ribboned parking lots that expressways have become, he can slide through the spaces, take off, go . . . And the kick is prodigious.

Instead of insulating its owner like a car, a bike extends him into the environment, all senses alert. Everything that happens on the road and in the air, the inflections of road surface, the shuttle and weave of traffic, the opening and squeezing of space, the cold and heat, the stinks, perfumes, noises and silences the biker flows into it in a state of heightened consciousness that no driver, with his windows and heater and radio, will ever know. It is this total experience, not the fustian clichés about symbolic penises and deficient father figures that every amateur Freudian trots out when motorcycles are mentioned, that creates bikers. Riding across San Francisco's Golden Gate Bridge on his motorcycle, the biker is sensually receptive to every yard of the way: to the bridge drumming under the tires, to the immense Pacific wind, to the cliff of icy blue space below.

'Se tu sarai solo,' Leonardo da Vinci remarked five hundred years ago, 'tu sarai tutto tuo' (If you are alone, you are your own man). Biking, like gliding, is one of the most delightful expressions of this fact. There is nothing second-hand or vicarious about the sense of freedom, which means possessing one's own and unique experiences, that a big bike well ridden confers. Antisocial? Indeed, yes. And being so, a means to sanity. The motorcycle is a charm against the Group Man.

ACKNOWLEDGEMENTS

I had always had the idea of an anthology of motorcycle writing circulating around my head but had never truly formulated the concept and collected the extracts together into a coherent flow. I have Trevor Dolby to thank for focusing my mind again and giving me the confidence to commence on the project. At the inspired suggestion of Stephen Esson I approached Bill Campbell at Mainstream Publishing. I'm grateful to Bill for taking the book on and all his colleagues in Edinburgh involved with the publication, particularly Fiona Atherton, Kate McLelland, Ailsa Bathgate, Seonaid MacLeod and Graeme Blaikie.

Friends and colleagues in the trade have been supportive throughout with their wise counsel in the office and over lunch: Paul Sidey, Will Sulkin, Tony Whittome, Suzanne Dean, Rowena Skelton-Wallace, Robin Robertson, Andy Hughes, Liz Sich, Dotti Irving, David Kent, Dan Franklin, Thomas Hughes-Hallett, Manoj Patel, Nandan Jha, Claire Ward, Alison Kaye, Tanya Dunbar, Christine Bergmann, Tracy Broderick, Paul Hicks and Nick White.

The clearance of permissions for a book of this type is a lengthy process and has been made that much easier by the guidance, support and language skills of Gemma Avery, Jonathan Sissons, Sarah McMahon, Sarah Wasley and Polly Collier. Judy Kennedy of Whitehorse Press was immensely helpful in securing the kind permission of the estate of Robert Fulton Jr. to extract from *One Man Caravan*. I am particularly grateful to Lucía Álvarez de Toledo for her charm, experience of the Latin American literary scene and sage advice. Her translation of the late Alberto Granado's account of his classic motorcycle journey with Che Guevara is utterly central to the structure of the book and was so generously donated. Mario Gómez of the Agencia Literaria Latinoamericana based in Havana was of great assistance in liaising with Alberto Granado's estate without which permission would simply not have been possible. I was fortunate enough to be introduced to Jim Perrin by my friend and recently retired colleague, Tony Whittome. In addition to kindly granting me permission to use his article, *Travels with a Harley*, Jim also directed me to the wonderful Don Whillans piece. Jim's highly regarded biography of Don Whillans, *The Villain* (Hutchinson, 2008), is a moving, authoritative and very entertaining study of this extraordinary maverick and *enfant terrible* of British mountaineering.

Posy Simmonds was particularly generous in donating the artwork that closes these acknowledgements.

As a production man I understand more than most that this book would simply not have been possible without the encouragement, expertise, hard work and generous support of the typesetters Craig Morrison and Alf Cuthbert at Palimpsest Ltd, the text designer Peter Ward, the paper suppliers Paul Tasker and Richard Selvey of Paper Management Services Ltd, Rob Slowe of Arctic Paper UK Ltd and finally the printers of the book Andy Simpson and Tony Chard of MPG Books Group Ltd.

I am indebted to you all.

PERMISSIONS